SUSAN D. SCHENCK

BACKYARD
SCIENCE &
DISCOVERY
WORKBOOK

NORTHEAST

ADVENTURE PUBLICATIONS

TABLE OF CONTENTS

ABOUT THIS BOOK

The Northeast is a wonderful, fascinating place. With 11 states and a vast range of habitats, plants, animals, and fungi, it has an amazing amount to observe and discover. Over the past 10 years, I've been lucky enough to explore the U.S. with students and friends, as a teacher, environmental educator, and naturalist. The natural communities of the Northeast have a special place in my heart, and I'm excited to be able to share them with you!

In this book, I want to fuel kids' curiosity for the natural world and get them outside observing nature in the Northeast. I hope that this workbook helps them learn to love and protect our natural spaces. This book can be a child's starting point for their own outdoor questions and discoveries. Once you start looking, there's so much to appreciate and observe, even in a nearby park or backyard!

I love what I do at work because it's what I do at home. When I'm not working, I'm usually outside: hiking, painting in my nature journal, learning new wildflowers, and volunteering for youth nature organizations.

This book features **23 hands-on science projects**, such as raising native caterpillars, making mushroom spore prints, and attracting moths and other insects with an ultraviolet light; **more than 20 simple, fun introductions** to the region's habitats, birds, seasons, and rocks and minerals; and more than **a dozen fun activities** to help you make hypotheses, observe nature, and learn about the world around you.

That's the fun part: you really never know what you're going to find on any given day. It's a little like a treasure hunt, and if you keep good records and share what you find, your observations can even help scientists learn more about the world, or even help you start off a career as a scientist.

So get outside, have fun, and share your discoveries!

Susan D. Schenck

GEOGRAPHY OF THE NORTHEAST

Covering areas known as New England and the Mid-Atlantic, the Northeast spans a huge area and includes 11 states. Practice your geography and label the states below. Bonus points if you can name the state capitals of each one.

Answers on page 158!

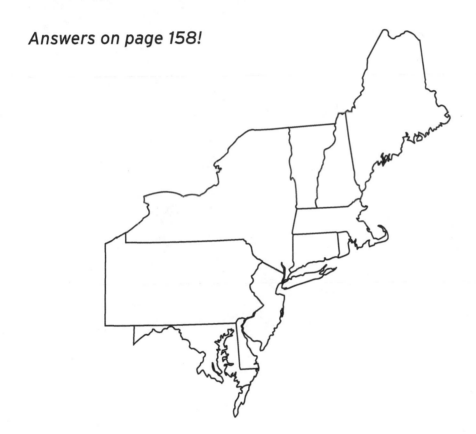

Connecticut (CT) _____

Delaware (DE) _____

Maine (ME) _____

Maryland (MD) _____

Massachusetts (MA) _____

New Hampshire (NH) _____

New Jersey (NJ) _____

New York (NY) _____

Pennsylvania (PA) _____

Rhode Island (RI) _____

Vermont (VT) _____

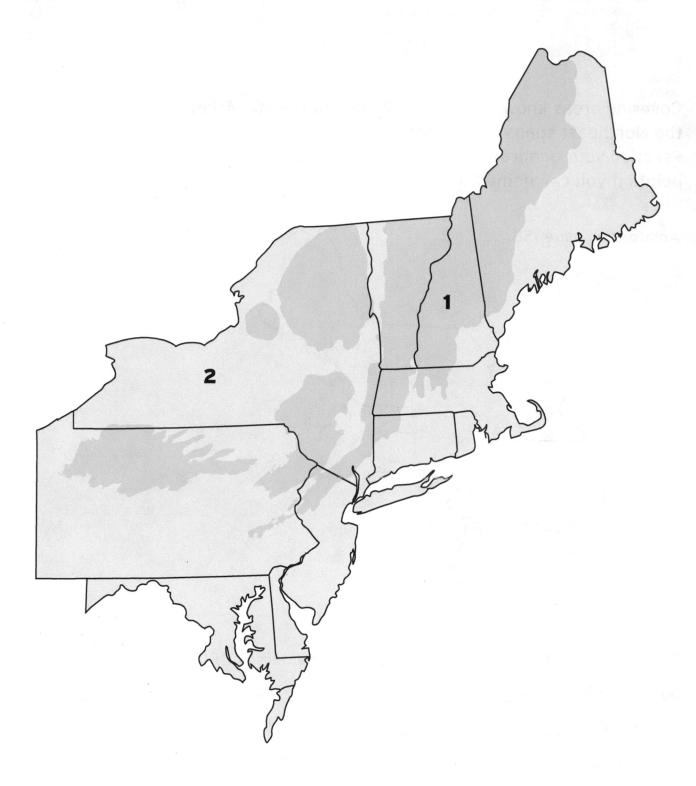

GET TO KNOW THE NORTHEAST'S BIOMES

The best way to get to know your Northeastern state—and your backyard—is by understanding the natural neighborhood it belongs to: its biome. A **biome** is a community of animals and plants that live in a specific kind of climate and environment.

You may have heard of some biomes before—like grasslands, forests, tundra, and so on.

The Northeast is home to two different biomes. (Numbers below correspond to the numbers on the map on the left.)

1. Coniferous Forests

2. Temperate Forests

You might be thinking, "Hey! Wait a minute, there are beaches in the Northeast!" And you're right. Beaches aren't their own biomes, though. For the most part, they're considered **ecosystems** instead of biomes. We'll go over the differences between a biome and an ecosystem later on in this section.

QUICK QUIZ

What kind of plant do both types of biomes have in common?

(**Hint:** *Forests have lots of them.*)

NORTHERN CONIFEROUS FORESTS

Coniferous forests are found in northern parts of the Northeast, where it's often cold and snowy in the winter. Coniferous forests, as their name suggests, have more conifer trees than the other biomes nearby.

A **conifer** is a tree that is **coniferous,** or has cones.

Another way to figure out if a tree is coniferous is by looking at the green parts coming off the branches. Conifers have needles or scaly structures coming out of the branches instead of leaves. Most conifers are **evergreen**, which means they don't lose their needles in the fall, but some conifers, like the Eastern Larch, are **deciduous,** meaning they do lose their needles seasonally. (When it comes to trees that aren't conifers, *deciduous* means they lose their leaves instead.)

QUICK QUIZ

Which of the following trees is evergreen?

A. Eastern Larch   B. Red Pine   C. Sugar Maple   D. American Beech

Answer on page 158!

1. Make a list of the evergreen trees near you.

_____

_____

_____

_____

2. What deciduous trees (trees that lose their needles or leaves) are nearby?

_____

_____

_____

_____

TEMPERATE FORESTS

The word **temperate** means "mild" or "moderate." In temperate forests, there are long periods over the summer where the weather is warm. These forests mostly have deciduous trees (trees that lose their leaves in the fall), such as oaks, beeches, and maples. Conifers can grow (or be planted) in temperate forests, although there aren't as many of them. Temperate forests are home to familiar animals, such as raccoons, woodpeckers, and White-Tailed Deer, but they also have thousands upon thousands of species of insects, fungi, and other plants.

QUICK QUIZ

There are many different kinds of trees in the Northeast's deciduous forests. Oaks, hickories, maples, and Tulip Poplars are common.

A tip for identifying trees: Observe the leaf edges. How would you describe them? Smooth? Bumpy? Lots of lobes ("fingers")? No lobes at all?

Can you identify each tree's leaves?

1. _____   2. _____   3. _____   4. _____

Answers on page 158!

1. How many different deciduous trees can you find near you?

_____

_____

_____

2. Which one is your favorite? Why?

_____

_____

_____

BEACHES & SALT MARSHES: IMPORTANT ECOSYSTEMS

I mentioned earlier that beaches are considered an ecosystem and not a biome. An **ecosystem** is all the interactions between living things (plants, animals, etc.) and non-living things (rocks, sand, etc.) in an area. Many different ecosystems make up a single biome. For example, in the temperate forest biome, you can have smaller ecosystems, such as a beach, or an area with a lot of maple trees, or a meadow in the middle of the forest, but all of these ecosystems are still part of the temperate forest biome. The whole area has similar groups of animals and plants living together in a specific kind of climate and environment.

Beaches are a pretty common ecosystem in the Northeast. All of the states in the Northeast have either ocean coastlines or lakeshores.

There are two main types of ocean beaches in the Northeast: rocky beaches, made up of big rocks, and sandy beaches, made of sand. In general, rocky beaches are found along the northern coast and gradually change to sandy beaches the farther south you travel. Rocky beaches are home to animals such as hermit crabs and sea anemones. Shorebirds are more likely to be found on sandy beaches.

Salt marshes are areas where fresh water from streams and rivers flows into the salt water in the ocean. These slow-moving areas make great spots for fish and other ocean creatures like crabs to lay their eggs. Birds (who like to eat the young fish) also build their nests in salt marshes.

In fact, a **threatened** bird called the Piping Plover builds its nest on sandy beaches in the Northeast. Piping Plovers are considered threatened because if more disappear, they would be endangered. Luckily, we can help. Can you guess some things that kids and adults are already doing to help Piping Plovers?

QUICK QUIZ

What might be helping Piping Plovers come back to the Northeast?

A. Kids staying out of the dunes and playing in the sand near the water instead

B. Government organizations protecting nests with roped-off areas

C. Families walking their dogs on a leash when they're on the beach

D. All of these things

Answer on page 158!

What other animals in your state are endangered or have been threatened?

_____

_____

_____

_____

THEN VS. NOW

The northeastern United States of today looks very different than it did 400 years ago. Back then, most of the land was covered by trees and contained vast areas of connected natural habitat, not a bunch of cities and natural areas like we have today. Huge hemlocks and pines grew in the forest, mixed in with a few pockets of grassland. Elk, bison, and mountain lions were common. Many Indigenous peoples moved seasonally in the region, some helping the local plant and wild-animal populations thrive by selectively burning the forest. On the coast, there were no boardwalks or modern cities.

European settlers began moving in during the 1600s, and this put the ecosystems in the Northeast under a lot of stress. Through the constant pressure on their natural resources, the biomes and ecosystems that Indigenous peoples depended on were severely harmed or outright destroyed. Nearly all forested areas in northeastern states like Pennsylvania were clear-cut. Only a few stands of virgin (untouched) remain, though third- and fourth-growth forests with a different combination of trees have grown in their place.

These intentional changes upended the ecosystems of the region, reducing or eliminating populations of the animals and plants that were important (or essential) to the traditional lifestyles of the Indigenous peoples of the Northeast. Americans are now beginning the hard work of coming together to repair relationships between Indigenous and European cultures, as well as mending our relationship with the natural world.

QUICK QUIZ

An animal that used to be common in an area but now is absent from it altogether is said to be **extirpated**. (*Extirpated* is different from *extinct*, because extirpated organisms can still live in other areas.) Which animals used to be common in the Northeast but are now rare or extirpated?

A. Mountain Lion

B. Wolves

C. Elk

D. Woodland Bison

E. All of them

Answer on page 158!

Elk were once found in the Northeast.

STATE SYMBOLS

Another good way to get to know the region is by learning your state's official symbols. From the state bird and flower, which you might know already, to lesser-known categories—such as state amphibian, gemstone, and even fossil—these well-known symbols are usually selected because they have a long history with the state. Of course, not every state has symbols for the same categories. Some states have a lot of symbols—even a state soil!—but others have just a handful. Still, they're a good way to learn about your state and its environment.

QUICK QUIZ

Some states use symbols that are **native** to their area. This means the plants, animals, and so on are found naturally living and growing in the area. Sometimes, state symbols are **nonnative** (not naturally found in that place). In the following list of six state symbols, only one is native to the northeastern United States. Which are they?

A. Honeybee (state insect of New Jersey, Vermont, and Maine)

B. White-Tailed Deer (state animal of Pennsylvania and New Hampshire)

C. Rhode Island Red Chicken (state bird of Rhode Island)

D. Peach Blossom (state flower of Delaware)

E. Lilac (state flower of New Hampshire and state bush of New York)

F. European Mantis (state insect of Connecticut)

Answer on page 158!

MARYLAND

Rockfish/Striped Bass
Fish

Diamondback Terrapin
Reptile

Black-Eyed Susan
Flower

White Oak
Tree

Baltimore Oriole
Bird

Baltimore Checkerspot
Insect

Maryland Blue Crab
Crustacean

Patuxent River Stone
Gem

Astrodon johnstoni
Dinosaur

Ecphora
(Ecphora gardnerae gardnerae)
Fossil Shell

STATE SYMBOLS

DELAWARE

Peach Blossom

Flower

American Holly

Tree

Sillimanite

Stone

Blue Hen

Bird

Belemnite

Fossil

Gray Fox

Wildlife Animal

Weakfish

Fish

Ladybug

Insect

Tiger Swallowtail

Butterfly

Channeled Whelk

Shell

Horseshoe Crab

Marine (Saltwater) Animal

NEW JERSEY

American Goldfinch

Bird

Violet

Flower

Hadrosaurus foulkii

Dinosaur

Red Oak

Tree

Bog Turtle

Reptile

Honeybee

Insect

Horse

Animal

Brook Trout

Fish

Knobbed Whelk

Shell

STATE SYMBOLS

NEW YORK

Eastern Bluebird

Bird

Rose

Flower

Sugar Maple

Tree

Garnet

Gem

Eurypterus remipes

Fossil

Beaver

Animal

Brook Trout

Fish

Ladybug

Insect

Snapping Turtle

Reptile

Bay Scallop

Shell

Lilac

Bush

PENNSYLVANIA

Ruffed Grouse

Bird

Mountain Laurel

Flower

Eastern Hemlock

Tree

White-Tailed Deer

Animal

Brook Trout

Fish

Firefly

Insect

Eastern Hellbender

Amphibian

STATE SYMBOLS

RHODE ISLAND

Rhode Island Red

Bird

Violet

Flower

Red Maple

Tree

Cumberlandite

Rock

Bowenite

Mineral

Striped Bass

Fish

Quahaug/Quahog

Shell

MASSACHUSETTS

Black-Capped Chickadee

Bird

Mayflower/ Ground Laurel/ Trailing Arbutus

Flower

American Elm

Tree

Roxbury Puddingstone

Rock

Rhodonite

Gemstone

Babingtonite

Mineral

Cod

Fish

Dinosaur Tracks

Fossil

Two-Spotted Lady Beetle

Insect

New England Neptune

Shell

Garter Snake

Reptile

STATE SYMBOLS

CONNECTICUT

American Robin

Bird

Mountain Laurel

Flower

Almandine Garnet

Mineral

Eubrontes

Fossil

Sperm Whale

Animal

European Mantis

Insect

American Shad

Fish

Eastern Oyster

Shellfish

VERMONT

Hermit Thrush
Bird

Red Clover
Flower

Sugar Maple
Tree

Granite, Marble, and Slate
Rock

Talc
Mineral

Grossular Garnet
Gem

Monarch
Butterfly

Northern Leopard Frog
Amphibian

Morgan Horse
Animal

Brook Trout
Cold Water Fish

Honeybee
Insect

STATE SYMBOLS

NEW HAMPSHIRE

Purple Finch
Bird

Purple Lilac
Flower

**White Birch/
Paper Birch**
Tree

Granite
Rock

Beryl
Mineral

Smoky Quartz
Gem

White-Tailed Deer
Animal

Ladybug
Insect

Karner Blue
Butterfly

Brook Trout
Freshwater Game Fish

**Pink Lady's
Slipper**
Wildflower

MAINE

Black-Capped Chickadee

Bird

White Pine Cone and Tassel

Flower

White Pine

Tree

Tourmaline

Mineral

Pertica quadrifaria

Fossil

Moose

Animal

Landlocked Salmon

Fish

Honeybee

Insect

Lobster

Crustacean

Wintergreen

Herb

Wild Blueberry

Berry

INTRODUCED VS. INVASIVE

Over the course of settlement of the Northeast, many plants and animals were **introduced** to the region. Some of these, such as peaches or horses, were introduced on purpose. Even though they are **nonnative**, they haven't been a problem. Other plants and animals reacted differently to their new home—once they got here, they spread quickly, often finding an environment with few predators. These species then became **invasive**, spreading uncontrollably and hurting native animals and plants. This term can apply to organisms (living things) that were introduced on purpose, or on accident.

A few familiar, but invasive, species:

Garlic Mustard

Earthworms
(in much of the Northeast)

Bush Honeysuckle

Oriental Bittersweet

Purple Loosestrife

House Sparrow

European Starling

Asian Shore Crab

QUICK QUIZ

Which of the following animals is an introduced species in the Northeast?

A. Black-Capped Chickadee

B. Sugar Maple Tree

C. Cow

D. Monarch Butterfly

Answer on page 158!

Can you think of other introduced species in your area?
Hint: Most farm animals aren't from here! The same is true for many weeds.

_____

_____

_____

_____

_____

_____

_____

_____

GETTING TO KNOW YOUR WEATHER

What's the **climate** like where you live? A region's climate is the long-term patterns in the **weather**. Weather is the day-to-day observations of temperature, rainfall or snowfall, cloud cover, and the like.

For example, if you live in a place that typically gets hot, muggy summers, and icy, slushy winters, that's your **climate.** If a hot summer day was 85 degrees and sunny, with a light breeze, that's your weather.

So, what is your climate like? Hot in the summer? Cooler in the summer? Snowy in the winter? Hardly any snow in the winter?

You probably know what a hot, sticky summer day is like, but what's the warmest you remember? Ninety degrees Fahrenheit, maybe 100°F? (**°F** is an abbreviation, or a shortcut, for writing the words "degrees Fahrenheit.")

What do you think the highest temperature ever recorded anywhere in your state was? (**Note:** It probably didn't reach this temperature in the place you live, but it did happen somewhere in your state.)

MAKE A HYPOTHESIS

Hypothesis: An "educated guess," based on things you already know.

1. Highest maximum temperature in my state?

My hypothesis/guess:

_____

2. You've felt cold, too, maybe shivering at the bus stop or walking to school. So what do you think the coldest temperature recorded anywhere in your state is?

My hypothesis/guess:

_____

3. And do you like building snow forts or having snowball fights? Me too! But what do you think the maximum amount of snow on the ground—anywhere in your state—was? Six inches? A foot? More?

My hypothesis/guess:

_____

_____

A FEW NORTHEAST WEATHER RECORDS

STATE NAME	HIGHEST TEMP (°F)	LOWEST TEMP (°F)	DEEPEST SNOW (INCHES)
Maryland	109° (1936)	-40° (1912)	54" (1993)
Delaware	110° (1930)	-17° (1893)	25" (2003)
New Jersey	110° (1936)	-34° (1904)	52" (1961)
New York	108° (1926)	-52° (1979)	119" (1943)
Pennsylvania	111° (1936)	-42° (1904)	60" (1958)
Rhode Island	104° (1975)	-28° (1942)	42" (1978)
Massachusetts	107° (1975)	-35° (1981)	62" (1996)
Connecticut	106° (1995)	-32° (1961)	55" (1961)
Vermont	107° (1912)	-50° (1933)	149" (1969)
New Hampshire	106° (1911)	-50° (1885)	164" (1969)
Maine	105° (1911)	-50° (2009)	84" (1969)

Data: ncdc.noaa.gov/extremes/scec/records

IS THE SUN SETTING EARLIER?!

In winter, you've probably noticed how it gets darker earlier. That happens because the earth is tilted on its axis, so certain parts of the planet get more daylight in some seasons than in others. If you've traveled to the north or to the south of where you live, you've probably noticed that the amount of daylight varies with **latitude,** or how far north or south you are of the equator. The time the sun sets (and rises) also varies with **longitude,** or how far east or west you are of the prime meridian.

MAKE A HYPOTHESIS

1. What month do you think has the shortest day of the year in the Northeast?

_____

2. Which month has the longest day of the year in the Northeast?

_____

3. On the shortest day of the year where you live, what time is sunset?

_____

LONGEST & SHORTEST DAYS
ACROSS THE NORTHEAST

The longest day of the year in the Northeast is known as the **summer solstice.** That's when the North Pole has its maximum tilt toward the sun. The shortest day in the Northeast is known as the **winter solstice,** when the North Pole is tilted away the most from the sun.

The date that each solstice occurs varies a little each year, but the summer solstice in the northern hemisphere always occurs between June 20 and June 22, and the winter solstice always occurs between December 20 and December 23.

On the winter solstice in 2030, this is when the sun will rise and set in several locations across the Northeast. The first city or town is in the far north; the second place is roughly in the middle of the region; and the third locale is in the far southern portion of the region. (The numbers following the name of each city or town are its latitude and longitude; see the previous page for an explanation.)

In far southern Maryland on the winter solstice, the sun rises at about the same time as in northern Maine, but it stays out nearly an hour later. The people in Maryland get another hour of daylight!

WINTER SOLSTICE

N. Maine (Caribou, 46.85, -68.00)
December 21
Sunrise: 7:13 a.m.
Sunset: 3:46 p.m.

Central New York (Syracuse, 43.05, -76.15)
December 21
Sunrise: 7:33 a.m.
Sunset: 4:33 p.m.

S. Maryland (Ocean City, 38.33, -75.09)
December 21
Sunrise: 7:14 a.m.
Sunset: 4:43 p.m.

Data: esrl.noaa.gov/gmd/grad/solcalc

The summer solstice sunset times in Maine and Maryland seem similar (8:29 p.m. compared with 8:27 p.m.).

Compare the time of the sunrise in southern Maryland to the time of sunrise in northern Maine. What do you notice?

This time, we're looking at places in the extreme east and far-west parts of the Northeast.

In eastern Massachusetts on the winter solstice, the sun rises about 40 minutes earlier and sets about 40 minutes earlier than in western Pennsylvania. The day lengths are similar; it's not like north-south differences that actually add to the hours of daylight a place gets.

Cape Cod, Massachusetts

SUMMER SOLSTICE

N. Maine (Caribou, 46.85, -68.00)
June 20
Sunrise: 4:38 a.m.
Sunset: 8:30 p.m.

S. Maryland (Ocean City, 38.33, -75.09)
June 20
Sunrise: 5:37 a.m.
Sunset: 8:27 p.m.

WINTER SOLSTICE

E. Massachusetts (near Wellfleet, 41.93, -70.00)
December 21
Sunrise: 7:05 a.m.
Sunset: 4:12 p.m.

North-Central Connecticut (north of Hartford, 41.93, -72.65)
December 21
Sunrise: 7:15 a.m.
Sunset: 4:23 p.m.

W. Pennsylvania (Near Erie, 41.93, -80.35)
December 21
Sunrise: 7:46 a.m.
Sunset: 4:54 p.m.

AVERAGE LAST FROST DATES

Eager to plant your garden? Before you get out and start planting, you have to keep the temperature in mind. If it gets too cold outside—especially overnight—the water inside the plants will freeze. Much like a water bottle or a can of soda that's been left in the freezer, the plants' cells explode and expand when they freeze. Exploded cells are, as you can imagine, not good for the plants, and they will get damaged or die altogether. When the plants die entirely, it's called a **killing frost.**

This is one reason that gardeners wait until the danger of a frost has passed to plant their flowers or crops in the ground. On the next page are the approximate dates of the last spring frosts across the Northeast. You'll notice that frost sticks around longer in areas with higher elevation, like mountainous western Maryland.

In Rhode Island, for example, cautious gardeners put their plants in the ground around Mother's Day, at the beginning of May.

Average last frost dates for the Northeast:

- **New York City and surrounding area, coastal New Jersey, a small area in eastern Pennsylvania, all of Delaware, and Eastern Maryland:** first two weeks of April

- **Coastal Massachusetts, southern Connecticut, all of Rhode Island, parts of New York near Lake Ontario, eastern and southern Pennsylvania, inland New Jersey, and most of western Maryland:** last two weeks of April

- **Southern Maine, New Hampshire, Vermont, and New York:** first two weeks of May

- **Northern and mountainous areas of Maine, New Hampshire, Vermont, New York, and small areas of northwestern Pennsylvania:** last two weeks of May

By the way, frost is one of the most interesting things to photograph in the winter!

GET TO KNOW THE SEASONS & THE WEATHER

Want to figure out the best time of year to do your favorite seasonal activities? For instance, when does the first snow typically fall? When do the first berries begin to ripen? When do the leaves fall off the trees?

The seasons of the year are like the hours on a clock: winter is the night, spring is the morning, summer is the afternoon, and fall is twilight. If you pay attention to this seasonal clock, along with the animals and plants found during each season, you'll be studying **phenology**. Phenology is the study of the cycles of the seasons and the natural world over time. By studying the phenology of your area—when certain birds arrive in spring, or when blueberries are first ripe in summer, or when the first inch of snow falls—you'll learn a lot about the natural world around you and what to expect next.

START OUT BY MAKING SOME PREDICTIONS

Before you start observing, see what you already know. Let's start with birds and insects. Sometimes people use robins and Monarchs as the first sign of the beginning of a new season. They're easier to spot during some months of the year.

American Robin

What season do you notice robins in the most?

_____

In which month?

_____

In which month(s) do you see Monarch Butterflies?

_____

Next, let's focus on plants.
In which months do the trees get their leaves where you live?

_____

When do they lose them?

_____

In which month do lilacs bloom where you live?

_____

Lilacs

Still plants, and these plants you can eat parts of:
When are blueberries ripe where you live?

_____

Do you have apple trees or crabapples nearby?

_____

In which season can you pick apples?

_____

Blueberries

Predictable weather events for the year:
When does it normally snow where you live?

_____

Which months does it never or rarely snow in?

_____

What time of year do you normally watch out for hurricanes?

_____

Apples

What time of year do you never or rarely get hurricanes?

_____

Monarch Butterfly

DO-IT-YOURSELF PHENOLOGY

The easiest way to start out with phenology is by observing one type of plant or animal throughout the year. Try this with the plants or animals in your yard. For example, if you have a maple tree or an oak tree nearby, observe it. Keep track of when it loses it leaves in the fall and then in the spring, when the buds poke out, flowers open, and leaves form, and when fruit (seeds or acorns) develops. Then keep track of when the tree loses its leaves. As you're recording your observations, jot down a few notes about the weather over the past few days. (**Note:** Your tree might do things in a different order. Maple trees often have flowers before they have leaves.)

It's easy to do: find a tree in your yard, and then write down the dates that you notice the following changes.

Year: _____

Buds form: _____

Flowers form: _____

Leaves emerge: _____

Seeds form:_____

Tree is fully "leafed out":_____

Leaves change colors in fall:_____

Leaves start falling off tree: _____

Then keep track of that same tree for a few years. See how different or similar those same dates are. Does the tree have buds the same day of each year? How about seeds? What was the weather like when these events happened?

Year: _____

Buds form: _____

Flowers form: _____

Leaves emerge: _____

Seeds form:_____

Tree is fully "leafed out":_____

Leaves change colors in fall:_____

Leaves start falling off tree: _____

RED MAPLE THROUGH THE SEASONS

PHENOLOGY CALENDAR: SPRING

These are the average months that these natural events occur. When these events happen can vary by year and by location, so keep track of when you spot these plants, animals, and events near you!

Remember, many states in the Northeast have mountains. Seasonal changes happen later in the mountains at higher elevations and earlier in areas near the Atlantic coast.

MARCH

- The last snow falls in central areas of the Northeast.
- The first Red-Winged Blackbirds arrive.
- American Robins start to be more noticeable.
- Ospreys return to their nesting sites on top of poles and trees.
- Ruffed Grouses drum to attract mates.
- Bears emerge from hibernation near the end of the month.
- Wood Frogs become active on warmer days. They still call even in slightly frozen ponds.
- Mourning Cloak butterflies also emerge on warm days. They spend the winter under tree bark as adults.
- Skunk Cabbage, a plant that can generate its own heat to melt snow, emerges in more-northern areas. It's already up in southern areas.
- Sugar Maple flower buds begin opening. They open later in more-northern and mountainous areas.

Red-Winged Blackbird

Skunk Cabbage

What I spotted in March:

_____

_____

APRIL

- Chickadees sing their "Fee-BEE, fee-BAY" song.
- Robins build nests.
- Ruby-Throated Hummingbirds begin to arrive near the end of the month.
- Barn Swallows return.
- Snowy Owls leave coastal areas.
- Painted Turtles begin to be visible and are already active in more-southern areas.
- Bumblebees start visiting flowers.
- Leaves begin to pop out on Sugar Maple trees.
- Near the end of the month, many maple trees are starting to produce **samaras** (also known as **helicopter seeds**).
- Larch trees' needles emerge (come out).
- Red Oaks' leaves emerge.
- Early wildflowers like trilliums and trout lilies begin to bloom.
- Dandelions grow, then flower.

What I spotted in April:

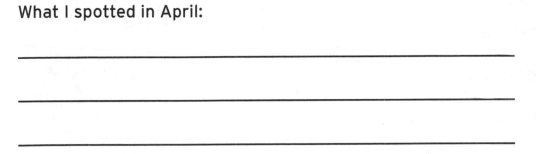

Sugar Maple Flower

Robin's Nest

Eastern Painted Turtle

White Trillium

MAY

- Warblers (a kind of songbird) migrate through, with many different colors, patterns, and songs.
- Baltimore Orioles return.
- Robins sit on their nests.
- Hummingbirds are active.
- Canada Geese have goslings (baby geese).
- Many kinds of turtles lay eggs.
- Snakes emerge from brumation (a type of hibernation where they are still active and not fully asleep).
- Swallowtail butterflies active.
- Lilacs bloom.
- Apple trees flower.
- Rhododendrons bloom at the end of the month.
- More forest-floor wildflowers bloom, including Mayapple and lady's slipper orchids.
- Milkweed begins to come up out of the ground.
- Morel mushrooms appear.

What I spotted in May:

_____

_____

_____

Lilac

Canada Goose

Eastern Tiger Swallowtail

Garter Snake

Morel

Pink Lady's Slipper

PHENOLOGY CALENDAR: SUMMER

JUNE

- Turkeys have poults (chicks).
- Wood Frog tadpoles turn into adults and emerge onto land.
- Gray Tree Frogs are chirping.
- Monarch Butterflies are active.
- Mayfly hatches start; some include so many insects that they can be seen on weather radar.
- Fireflies (lightning bugs) are visible.
- Dragonfly adults emerge, and you can sometimes see dozens at a time.
- Periodical Cicadas hatch every 13–17 years. (Depending on how old you are, you might not have seen one yet!)
- Blueberry bushes are flowering.
- Horseshoe Crabs are very active: it's mating season.

What I spotted in June:

_____

_____

_____

Monarch Butterfly

Springtime Darner

Firefly

Wild Turkey

Periodical Cicada

JULY

- American Goldfinches build nests.
- Adult Dog-Day Cicadas (green and black) are singing; you may also find the papery exoskeletons they leave behind. They emerge every year.
- Blueberries, huckleberries, and raspberries are ripe.
- Wildflowers growing in meadows are blooming.

What I spotted in July:

_____

_____

_____

American Goldfinch

Blueberries

AUGUST

- Flocks of Sanderlings and other shorebirds return to coastal areas.
- Clearwing Moth and other sphinx moths are active.
- Ghost Pipe flowers bloom. These small, colorless plants get their nutrients from fungi that live in tree roots.
- Cardinal Flowers bloom.
- Sunflowers are blooming.

What I spotted in August:

_____

_____

_____

Clearwing Moth

Ghost Pipe

PHENOLOGY CALENDAR: FALL

SEPTEMBER

- Hawks begin to migrate south.
- Woodchucks begin their fall feast to prepare for winter hibernation.
- Gray Squirrels are busy caching (hiding) acorns for winter.
- Moose and elk more visible in northern areas: it's their mating season.
- Monarch Butterflies migrate to Mexico.
- Sumac leaves are turning red.
- Poison Ivy leaves turn yellow or red (don't touch!).
- Goldenrod flowers and asters are visible everywhere, often along roadsides.
- Acorns start dropping from oaks.
- Lots of mushroom activity, including the famously stinky stinkhorn.

Gray Squirrel

Sumac

Poison Ivy

Goldenrod

What I spotted in September:

_____

_____

_____

OCTOBER

- Dark-Eyed Juncos begin to arrive.
- Harlequin Ducks arrive to the coasts to spend the winter.
- Ospreys migrate south.
- Snakes go into brumation and are less active.
- Dragonflies leave and migrate south.
- Woolly Bear Caterpillars are active and spend the winter as larvae.
- Deciduous trees turn colors, and the leaves fall off later in the month.
- Eastern Larch needles turn orange.
- Witch Hazel bushes bloom.

What I spotted in October:

Dark-Eyed Junco

Harlequin Duck

_____

_____

_____

NOVEMBER

- Most migrating songbirds have long since left.
- Snowy Owls arrive at coastal spots in the northern part of the Northeast.
- Short-Tailed and Long-Tailed Weasels molt (shed and regrow their fur, usually in a different color) from brown backs and white bellies to being entirely white. In the southern portions of the region, weasels stay brown all year.
- Eastern Larch needles fall off.

What I spotted in November:

Snowy Owl

Short-Tailed Weasel

_____

_____

_____

PHENOLOGY CALENDAR: WINTER

DECEMBER

- Average month of first 1-inch snowfall in much of the region.
- Winter finches, like crossbills and Evening Grosbeaks, arrive.
- Bears hibernate once temps are consistently below freezing.

What I spotted in December:

_____

_____

Black Bear

JANUARY

- It's the snowiest and coldest month in much of the region.
- Bald Eagles move to rivers along the coast to fish.
- Great Horned Owls call for mates and lay eggs.
- Foxes mark territory with stinky pee during mating season.

What I spotted in January:

_____

_____

Echo Lake

FEBRUARY

- Great Horned Owl chicks hatch.
- Killdeers (a shorebird) arrive late in the month.
- Maple sap (used to make maple syrup) begins to run.

What I spotted in February:

_____

_____

Maple Sap

YOUR STATE'S MAJOR FARM CROPS & FARM PRODUCTS

After settlement, much of the Northeast became farmland. A wide variety of crops and products is grown in the Northeast, from apples in New York and blueberries in New Jersey to the chickens raised in Delaware and Maryland. These are the top crops, or **commodities** (agricultural products), in the Northeast.

DELAWARE

- Broiler Chickens
- Corn
- Other Crops
- Soybeans
- Chicken Eggs

MARYLAND

- Broiler Chickens
- Corn
- Other Crops
- Soybeans
- Dairy Products/Milk

NEW JERSEY

- Other Crops
- Flowers
- Blueberries
- Bell Peppers
- Other Animal Products

NEW YORK

- Dairy Products/Milk
- Other Crops
- Corn
- Cattle
- Apples

PENNSYLVANIA

- Dairy Products/Milk
- Cattle
- Other Crops
- Broiler Chickens
- Corn

RHODE ISLAND

- Other Crops
- Other Animal Products
- Chicken Eggs
- Turkeys
- Dairy Products/Milk

MASSACHUSETTS

- Other Crops
- Cranberries
- Other Animal Products
- Dairy Products/Milk
- Turkeys

CONNECTICUT

- Other Crops
- Flowers
- Dairy Products/Milk
- Other Animal Products
- Chicken Eggs

VERMONT

- Dairy Products/Milk
- Other Crops
- Cattle
- Maple Products
- Hay

NEW HAMPSHIRE

- Other Crops
- Dairy Products/Milk
- Chicken Eggs
- Turkeys
- Cattle

MAINE

- Other Crops
- Potatoes
- Dairy Products/Milk
- Other Animal Products
- Chicken Eggs

QUICK QUIZ

If you haven't lived near a farm or worked on one, you might not recognize the crops growing in the field. Can you identify each type of crop?

1. _____

2. _____

3. _____

4. _____

5. _____

Answers on page 158!

WILDFLOWERS

State symbols are just some of the wildflowers in the Northeast. In fact, the region is famous for its spring forest flowers. **Note:** Please don't pick wildflowers—instead, take pictures or make a drawing.

SPRING FLOWERS

Sessile Trillium

White Trillium

Trout Lily

Canada Mayflower

Bloodroot

Starflower

Mayapple

Dutchman's Breeches

Pink Lady's Slipper

Wild Columbine

Jack-in-the-Pulpit

SUMMER AND FALL FLOWERS

Goldenrod

New York Aster

Yarrow

Ghost Pipe

Joe-Pye Weed

Queen Anne's Lace
(Wild Carrot)

Do not pick. *Queen Anne's Lace looks like Poison Hemlock, which is very poisonous, and these two plants are hard to tell apart.*

QUICK QUIZ

Which of these state flowers or plants is native to the Northeast?

A. Peach Blossom

B. Lilac

C. Mountain Laurel

Answer on page 158!

COASTAL PLANTS

Lots of cities in the Northeast are along the coastline of the Atlantic Ocean, so we should talk about coastal plants too! While they may not be as showy as woodland wildflowers, they play important parts in their habitats.

American Beachgrass

Northern Bayberry

Beach Heather

Beach Plum

Beach Pea

Glasswort

Saltmarsh Cordgrass

Eel Grass

BLOW BUBBLES WITH A TREE

Trees need to be able to carry water from their roots to their leaves. They also need to be able to carry sugar from their leaves to their roots. This means that trees are full of "pipes" to carry this water and sugar. The "pipes" are actually specialized plant parts called **vascular tissue.** In any case, you can see these pipes in action by blowing bubbles with a piece of a tree. Try it out!

WHAT YOU'LL NEED

- Liquid soap
- A slice of a dry tree branch, about half an inch thick. It will look like a huge coin or a cookie. You can buy a slice at a craft store, or you can ask an adult to saw off a slice for you. Make sure that your branch is dry and has been off the tree for a few weeks.
- Water
- Optional: paper towel or thin cloth

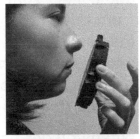

WHAT TO DO

Put a few drops of liquid soap on one side of the branch slice. Sprinkle a little water on top, or run the slice gently under the faucet. You want just enough water to get it wet, but not enough to wash the soap off.

Put your mouth on the not-soapy side of the branch slice. If you don't want to put your mouth on a branch, put a thin piece of cloth or a paper towel over it first. Now blow into the tree slice. (You might have to blow really hard!) Eventually, you should see foamy bubbles pouring out the other side.

What happens if you try this with a rock? Why does the tree slice let air through for bubbles but not the rock?

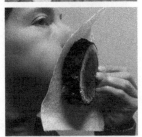

MAKE A LEAF SUNCATCHER

Bring home some colorful fall leaves, and display them in your window.

WHAT YOU'LL NEED

- Some dry leaves

- Two pieces of self-sealing lamination sheets or clear contact paper. Each piece should be at least as big as a sheet of paper. You can find contact paper and lamination sheets in the supplies section of an office products store. Lamination sheets are easier to work with but harder to find. For the example here, I used lamination sheets.

- Optional: Clear tape

WHAT TO DO

With an adult, or an adult's permission, go out and collect some dry leaves. It's best to choose from things that you know are safe to touch: oaks, maples, grass, and so on. If you're not sure if you can touch it, leave it alone or ask an adult. That way, you can avoid poison ivy, poison oak, poison sumac, and anything else that can make you itchy or sick.

When you get back home, it's time to arrange your leaves. Make sure the amount of space your leaves covers is only the size of one of your pieces of contact paper or sheeting.

Arrange your leaves the way you like them, so they're easy to stick on your paper when it's time.

Next, get your lamination sheet or contact paper ready. Peel off the paper backing to uncover the sticky side. This can be tricky! Once you peel off the paper backing, the clear part can get stuck to itself. You might have to ask someone to help you keep the clear part straightened out.

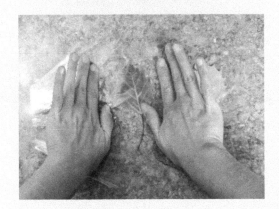

Lay out the lamination sheet or contact paper sticky-side up. Press the leaves on the sticky side so they stay put.

Once you're done, peel off the back of your second piece of sheeting or contact paper. Place this second piece sticky-side down over your leaves, sandwiching your leaves in between the layers. You might have to press on the top piece a little to get the air bubbles out.

Optional: Use clear tape to hang your finished leaf suncatcher in a window.

WHAT'S THE HIGHEST & LOWEST POINT IN YOUR STATE?

The Northeast covers a lot of land, from Maryland beaches to Maine mountains. Just how tall are those towering New England peaks, anyway? When measuring a state's elevation, or that of a mountain or a hill, geographers compare a given place's elevation with the elevation at sea level. So for example, Florida's highest point—in the entire state—is only 345 feet above sea level. That's not exactly surprising, as it's surrounded by ocean.

What do you think the highest point is in your state? What about the lowest?

Highest: _____ feet above sea level

Lowest: _____ feet above sea level

FAST FACT

Visiting the highest point in an area is something of a growing hobby. Known as **highpointing,** it's a fun way to get to know your state, and its quirks, a little better. Though in some places, such as Alaska, where the highest point is 20,310 feet, you'll definitely need a lot of experience, gear, and training before you ever make an attempt.

Data: www.usgs.gov/science-support/osqi/yes/resources-teachers/highest-and-lowest-elevations

DELAWARE

**Highest Point
Above Sea Level:**

448 feet
*DE-PA state line,
New Castle County*

**Lowest Point
Above Sea Level:**

0 feet
Atlantic Ocean

MARYLAND

**Highest Point
Above Sea Level:**

3,360 feet
*Hoye-Crest,
Garrett County*

**Lowest Point
Above Sea Level:**

0 feet
Atlantic Ocean

NEW JERSEY

**Highest Point
Above Sea Level:**

1,803 feet
*High Point,
Sussex County*

**Lowest Point
Above Sea Level:**

0 feet
Atlantic Ocean

NEW YORK

**Highest Point
Above Sea Level:**

5,344 feet
*Mount Marcy,
Essex County*

**Lowest Point
Above Sea Level:**

0 feet
Atlantic Ocean

*highest locations shown for each state

HIGHEST & LOWEST POINTS

PENNSYLVANIA

Highest Point
Above Sea Level:

3,213 feet
*Mount Davis,
Somerset County*

Lowest Point
Above Sea Level:

0 feet
*Delaware River,
Delaware County*

RHODE ISLAND

Highest Point
Above Sea Level:

812 feet
*Jerimoth Hill,
Providence County*

Lowest Point
Above Sea Level:

0 feet
Atlantic Ocean

MASSACHUSETTS

Highest Point
Above Sea Level:

3,491 feet
*Mt. Greylock,
Berkshire County*

Lowest Point
Above Sea Level:

0 feet
Atlantic Ocean

CONNECTICUT

Highest Point
Above Sea Level:

2,380 feet
*Mount Frissell,
Litchfield County*

Lowest Point
Above Sea Level:

0 feet
Long Island Sound

VERMONT

Highest Point
Above Sea Level:

4,393 feet
*Mount Mansfield,
Chittenden County*

Lowest Point
Above Sea Level:

95 feet
Lake Champlain

NEW HAMPSHIRE

Highest Point
Above Sea Level:

6,288 feet
*Mount Washington,
Coos County*

Lowest Point
Above Sea Level:

0 feet
Atlantic Ocean

MAINE

Highest Point
Above Sea Level:

5,268 feet
*Mount Katahdin,
Piscataquis County*

Lowest Point
Above Sea Level:

0 feet
Atlantic Ocean

*highest locations shown for each state

SPOT YOUR STATE BIRD

AMERICAN GOLDFINCH

State Bird of New Jersey

WHEN WILL I SEE THEM?
They're found year-round in the Northeast, with especially high numbers in the spring and summer. You may recognize them from their call, which sounds like they're saying "Potato chip! Potato chip!"

WILL THEY COME TO MY YARD?
Yes! Goldfinches eat seeds, and they aren't exactly picky about what kind, though they love sunflower seeds and nyjer seed (which is often sold in ready-made "socks" to hang outside).

AMERICAN ROBIN

State Bird of Connecticut

WHEN WILL I SEE THEM?
Robins are most obvious in spring through fall, when they are easy to spot hopping around yards, looking for worms and bugs. In all parts of the Northeast, they often stick around during the winter, but they're harder to find. In the northernmost parts of the Northeast (northern Maine, New Hampshire, and Vermont), they become the most scarce (hard to find). Robins are harder to spot in the winter because they have to resort to other food sources, such as fruit still clinging to winter trees. On cold days, you can sometimes see them perched in trees, all fluffed up to stay warm.

WILL THEY COME TO MY YARD?
Maybe. Robins don't come to birdseed feeders, but they will sometimes come to suet (animal fat) feeders in the winter. If you really want to attract them, leave out fruit or mealworms.

BLACK-CAPPED CHICKADEE

State Bird of Massachusetts and Maine

WHEN WILL I SEE THEM?
Black-Capped Chickadees are very common in much of the Northeast. In fact, you might even recognize their familiar "Chick-a DEE-DEE-DEE" call. Another kind of chickadee, the Carolina Chickadee, lives in southern parts of the Northeast.

You can usually identify a chickadee based on where you are: if you're in the northern Northeast, it's Black-Capped; in the southern Northeast, its Carolina. In the middle? Could be either one.

WILL THEY COME TO MY YARD?
Yes! Black-Capped Chickadees love all kinds of bird food: black sunflower seeds, suet, nyjer seeds, even peanut butter!

EASTERN BLUEBIRD

State Bird of New York

WHEN WILL I SEE THEM?
Bluebirds are found throughout the Northeast in the summer, although they're more common in some areas, and in some seasons, than others. Eastern Bluebirds are common in the spring and summer in New York, Pennsylvania, and parts of Vermont. They're still around in other places, so keep an eye out!

WILL THEY COME TO MY YARD?
Maybe. These birds don't come to seed feeders, but they love to eat mealworms, so if you put some wiggly worms in a dish, they might show up. The best way to get Eastern Bluebirds to visit is to put up a nesting box for them.

SPOT YOUR STATE BIRD

BALTIMORE ORIOLE

State Bird of Maryland

WHEN WILL I SEE THEM?
This bird is found from late April to the middle of October throughout much of the Northeast (although some individual birds stick around longer). The bright-orange-and-black males (and brownish-orange-and-dark-brown females) visit fruit trees and bushes in yards and in the wild.

WILL THEY COME TO MY YARD?
They could. It depends on if you have any fruit in your yard.

Baltimore Orioles love to eat ripe fruit, especially reddish- or orange-colored fruit. You can hang orange halves from the trees (or rest them on a railing) to invite orioles into your yard.

BLUE HEN

State Bird of Delaware

WHEN WILL I SEE THEM?
Blue Hens are domesticated (tame) chickens. You'll find them on farms, or maybe in the yard of a neighbor who raises chickens.

WILL THEY COME TO MY YARD?
Not unless you have chickens!

RUFFED GROUSE

State Bird of Pennsylvania

WHEN WILL I SEE THEM?
Ruffed Grouse are more common in the mountainous and northern areas of the Northeast. They don't live in Delaware and do live only in the most western tip of Maryland. In places with higher elevations and farther north, you're more likely to see or hear grouse in April, when they perform their complicated and fancy courtship displays.

WILL THEY COME TO MY YARD?
Not likely, but maybe if you live in a rural area in the mountains of the Northeast. These wild relatives of the chicken are easily startled, and they stick to more-wild areas.

RHODE ISLAND RED

State Bird of Rhode Island

WHEN WILL I SEE THEM?
Rhode Island Reds are domesticated (tame) chickens. You'll find them on farms, or maybe in the yard of a neighbor who raises chickens. They're a common breed with an all-over rusty red color. The roosters have shiny, greenish-black tails.

WILL THEY COME TO MY YARD?
Not unless you have chickens!

SPOT YOUR STATE BIRD

HERMIT THRUSH

State Bird of Vermont

WHEN WILL I SEE THEM?

Hermit Thrushes are known for their flute-like song in the mountains and hills of the northern Northeast. In the summer, you can find hermit thrushes in mountainous areas of Pennsylvania, New York, Massachusetts, Vermont, New Hampshire, and Maine. In the winter, you're more likely to find them in Delaware and Maryland.

WILL THEY COME TO MY YARD?

Not likely. Hermit thrushes like mountainous, forested areas. If you happen to live in a mountainous area in the northern Northeast, you could try leaving out fruit or mealworms.

PURPLE FINCH

State Bird of New Hampshire

WHEN WILL I SEE THEM?

A Purple Finch was once described as "a sparrow dipped in raspberry juice." From that description, you can probably guess that they're a reddish-brownish-pink color. The berry coloring on a Purple Finch goes over the head, cheeks, back, and even above the tail.

Purple Finches are seen year-round in most of the Northeast. They're most common in the fall and winter.

WILL THEY COME TO MY YARD?

It's possible! Purple Finches can be shy, and other birds, like House Finches and House Sparrows, can scare them away. Purple Finches love seeds, especially black sunflower seeds.

1. Have you spotted your state bird? Where?

_____

_____

_____

_____

2. What's your favorite state bird in the Northeast?

_____

_____

_____

3. How about your favorite bird in your state?

_____

_____

_____

MAKE YOUR YARD BIRD-FRIENDLY

Lawns are pretty, but they don't do a lot to help birds, bugs, and most other kinds of wildlife. To really draw birds (and the insects they often eat!) to your yard, you and your parents can make your yard a bit wilder. It's pretty easy to start doing this. Here are a few tips:

Wild Geranium

PLANT NATIVE PLANTS

Whether you're planting native trees that provide cover, nesting sites, or fruit, or sunflowers that become snacking stations once they droop forward in late summer and fall, native plants are beacons to birds. For a list of what to plant, visit www.audubon.org/native-plants. To make sure you're finding the best native plants, look for a native-plant nursery near where you live.

Butterflyweed

PUT OUT A WATER SOURCE

Birds don't just need food—they need water too! A bird bath, especially one with a "water wiggler" (available at many birding or home improvement stores), is a great option. The movement of the water prevents mosquitoes from laying eggs in the water, and the sound of the moving water draws in birds from all over.

Cardinal Flower

DON'T SPRAY YOUR YARD WITH BUG OR WEED KILLERS

Mosquitoes are really annoying, but the popular foggers or sprays that many people apply to their yards don't just kill mosquitoes. These insecticides often kill any bugs they touch, including bees, butterflies, and the many beetles and other creepy-crawlies that birds depend on for food. Pesticides and herbicides (weed killers) can also directly hurt birds.

Birdbath

LEAVE OUT NEST-MAKING MATERIALS IN SPRING

Bird nests are pretty incredible, and it's even more impressive that birds make them using only their feet and their beaks!

WHAT TO DO

You can help them out by leaving natural, pesticide-free nesting materials in handy locations around your yard. Examples include soft, fluffy plant parts, such as the down from cattails, moss, or feathers you find on the ground (but make sure to wear gloves when picking those up). You can put these in easy-to-access places around your yard; on the ground, wedged into tree bark—or even hanging in an empty suet feeder.

Important Note: There are some things you don't want to give birds, especially human-made or synthetic products such as plastic, metal, or dryer lint. This includes most strings and yarns. And even though it came from our heads, no human hair or pet hair, please! Birds can get their feet and other body parts trapped in strings and hair, and dryer lint makes their nests too soggy when it rains. Human-made materials can also be **toxic** (poisonous) to birds, either if the bird eats some of these materials or if it absorbs some of the chemicals in the materials.

Cattail fluff is often used in bird nests.

MAKE A RECIPE TO FEED TO BIRDS

If you get creative, you can feed birds a lot more than birdseed! Making your own bird food is a fun way to attract the birds you want to see.

Here are two options, although there are lots of others.

DO-IT-YOURSELF BIRDSEED MIX

A lot of the birdseed mixes sold in stores just aren't very good. Often, they contain lots of filler seeds (such as milo, a small, brown, round seed). Filler seeds don't have a lot of the nutrients that birds need, unlike seeds such as black-oil sunflower seeds, which are full of good stuff like protein, vitamins, and fats.

So what do you do? Make your own birdseed mix! Buy some black-oil sunflower seeds to use as your base, then add other seeds to those.

Here's a mix that works great for platform feeders. All of the ingredients are usually available at garden centers or home improvement stores.

WHAT YOU'LL NEED

• 4 cups black-oil sunflower seeds

• 1 cup peanut chips

• 1 cup cracked corn

WHAT TO DO

Mix it all together and place it on a hanging bird feeder. For an extra-tasty treat, you can also add in some sliced apples or plums.

A SIMPLE PEANUT BUTTER BIRDSEED FEEDER

WHAT YOU'LL NEED

- Pine cones
- Peanut butter
- Black-oil sunflower seeds or a birdseed mix
- Some string

WHAT TO DO

This tried-and-true recipe really works. First, you'll need to collect some pine cones. Then mix some peanut butter and sunflower seeds in a bowl. Next, take the pine cones and push them into the peanut butter and seeds, making sure everything is mixed together well like in the picture. Now tie some string to the top of each pine cone, and hang it from a tree. You can do this as many times as you like.

If you can't find any pine cones, just mix the ingredients together, then "paint" or smear the mixture onto a tree's bark.

Make both kinds of feeders, then keep track of the birds that come to each one! Did different birds come to the different feeders?

_____

_____

_____

DO A BACKYARD BIRD COUNT

If you're new to birding, chances are you probably haven't conducted a backyard bird count before. You can count birds in your yard, in a park, or even from a parking lot. You can do a bird count with a group of family or friends, or, if it's OK with the adults in your life, you can do one by yourself. It's a simple activity, but it can teach you and your friends quite a bit about birds, including how to recognize their calls and when and where to look. It's also a lot of fun, and you might be surprised at what you find. Best of all, you don't need any gear at all, though a field guide to birds, binoculars, and a smartphone camera can be handy.

WHAT YOU'LL NEED

• A notepad and a pen or pencil, to record your finds

• A field guide, binoculars, and a smartphone camera (optional)

WHAT TO DO

To conduct your count, pick a 15-minute time slot for everyone to look for birds. Go to your backyard (or even a balcony) with a notepad and something to write with, and quietly look and listen for birds. Look near feeders, if you have them; see if you can spy birds flitting about in cover or perched in trees, and especially near garden areas. Even potted plants or container gardens sometimes have birds like House Finches in them.

Wherever you are, but especially in the city or the suburbs, look for birds soaring overhead. A place where lots of people live might not seem like a birding hot spot, but because major cities usually are near rivers, have tall buildings, and have plenty of pigeons and songbirds, they're often home to nesting groups of birds like Peregrine Falcons, which hunt the other birds for food.

When someone spots a bird, point it out—again, quietly—and try to snag a zoomed-in photo. (It doesn't have to be perfect, just enough to help with identification.) Then record what kind of birds they are, if you recognize them, how many birds you spotted, and what they were doing. If you don't recognize a bird and didn't get a picture of it, sketch out a quick drawing or make notes about its appearance, color, and size. Then you can check a field guide or photos online to try to identify it.

BIRD SOUNDS

You may hear a bird without seeing it; this will happen more than you'd think. If you recognize the call, mark it down and add it to your count. If you don't know the call (again, this will happen pretty often), try to remember what it sounds like—that could mean writing down a description or using a recording app on a smartphone. To narrow down what your bird could be, head online to a website like **All About Birds** (www.allaboutbirds.org), and listen to recordings of birds that could help you figure it out.

Fun Fact: People who enjoy observing birds call themselves **birders** in the U.S. Getting to know birds involves learning about their sounds and their behavior, not just looking at them for their colors or shapes.

RECORD YOUR FINDS

After you're done counting birds for 15 minutes, combine all of your finds into a list. Consider setting up an account on a community science site such as **eBird** (www.ebird.org; with an adult's permission, of course). There, you can create a "life list" of species spotted over time, and you'll also contribute to  science—the resulting maps help create a snapshot of bird life over time. Ornithologists (scientists who study birds), other scientists, and birders use the info that community members (like you, maybe!) put in to contribute to new bird discoveries.

DO A BACKYARD BIRD COUNT

THE CHRISTMAS BIRD COUNT

Once you get the hang of doing a bird count, consider participating in a national one. There are two long-running bird counts. One is The Christmas Bird Count, which has been around for 120 years. It takes place from mid-December to early January, and volunteers spread out to count birds in specific areas around each state and the country, with counts occurring in each local area for only one day. Christmas Bird Counts are often an adventure that lasts several hours, so if you want to join in on the fun, tell your parents and prepare ahead of time! To find out more, visit www.audubon.org/conservation/science/christmas-bird-count.

THE GREAT BACKYARD BIRD COUNT

This bird count is similar to the Christmas Bird Count, but The Great Backyard Bird Count happens everywhere on the same dates in February. You can participate if you spot birds for as little as 15 minutes, making it easy to join. For more information and to sign up, visit www.birdcount.org.

THE BIG SIT

This bird count happens every October. It's a little different from the other two—instead of walking around a large area, you stay in one spot. All observations for The Big Sit must be made from inside a circle no more than 17 feet in diameter (across from side to side). You can stay all day or just show up for part of a Big Sit. To learn more or find an event in your area, visit www.thebigsit.org.

Keep track of the birds you see or spot here!

_____

_____

_____

_____

PLANT A HUMMINGBIRD, BEE & BUTTERFLY GARDEN

One way you can help wildlife wherever you live is by making your area a bit wilder. The easiest way to do that is to plant native plants. You don't need a huge amount of space to do this; even a small container garden with native plants can help attract—and feed—pollinators.

WHAT TO DO

Here are a few examples of how to attract some of the more sought-after pollinators:

• Common sunflowers are easy to grow (sometimes they grow by themselves when birds drop seeds), and they attract bumblebees, flies, and colorful beetles. Read the back of the seed package to see how tall your sunflowers will grow—if they grow more than 4 feet tall, they will do better in the ground than they will in a container.

• Planting milkweed (Common Milkweed, Butterfly Milkweed, Pink Swamp Milkweed, Showy Milkweed) attracts Monarch Butterflies. The females lay their eggs on the plant, and the caterpillars munch away on the milkweed (you can spot them if you take a close look).

• Plants with long tubular flowers, such as Wild Bergamot and native-Northeast Trumpet Honeysuckle, attract hummingbirds and sphinx moths (large moths that are sometimes mistaken for hummingbirds).

• Let the "weeds" be: dandelions, Common Blue Violets, and plants like White Clover provide bees, butterflies, and other beneficial insects with needed resources. Plus, not only are these plants pretty and great to walk on (clover doesn't get crunchy like turfgrass does), but they're tough and easy to care for.

For a dedicated list, see this excellent write-up at the website for the Xerces Society: www.xerces.org/pollinator-conservation/pollinator-friendly-plant-lists.

Once you plant your hummingbird, bee, and butterfly garden, keep track of the insects and birds you spot here!

_____

_____

_____

_____

_____

_____

SET UP A
WINDOW FEEDER

If you want to get an up-close look at birds, put up a window feeder. These transparent ledge-style feeders attach to a window with suction cups, and once the birds get used to the feeder and your presence on the other side of the glass, birds will chow down, enabling you to watch them from almost no distance at all.

BIRD NEST CAMS

For a different kind of up-close look at birds, head online and look at the many different nest cams offered on various bird sites. There are online nest cams for eagles hawks, ospreys, even hummingbirds.

For a list, visit www.allaboutbirds.org/cams.

MAKE YOUR WINDOWS SAFER FOR BIRDS

Hundreds of millions of birds are killed or injured each year when they accidentally fly into windows, often because they saw a reflection of nearby plants or the sky and thought it was a safe place to fly. Such collisions are often deadly, and they are a constant problem.

WHAT TO DO

There are a few simple safety steps you can take to help:

1. Close your blinds or curtains—this will make the window look more like a barrier. This is very important at night, when a lit-up room might seem like a welcoming place for a bird to fly.

2. When placing bird feeders, either keep them far away from windows (more than 20 feet) or keep them very close to windows—either directly on the window, using suction cups, or just a few feet away. (Even if a bird flies into a window from a close-by feeder, it won't fly fast enough to get seriously hurt.)

3. Consider using "scare tape" or "flash tape"—reflective ribbons in iridescent colors that birds don't like. These can be effective in keeping birds away from your windows.

4. Make birds more wary of your windows by placing ribbons, pinwheels, and other moving accessories in front of them. This can scare birds away.

5. Keep plants away from windows, as birds often mistake them for part of the natural scenery outdoors.

WILDLIFE REHABILITATION NEAR YOU

If you see an animal get hurt or find one that you know is injured, put your pets indoors, then contact your local wildlife rehabilitation center or a permit-carrying wildlife rehabilitation expert. To find one, check the website for your state's department of natural resources or department of fish and wildlife. (This department is named something slightly different depending on the state, so you may have to use different wording.)

WHAT TO DO

If you find what you think is an orphaned baby animal and it's in a safe spot, don't pick it up. Instead, call your local wildlife rehabilitation center first—the animal actually might not be orphaned at all (its parents may be nearby or gathering food), and handling or disturbing the animal might actually harm it.

When in doubt, leave an injured animal alone and call an expert. When animals are hurt, they are scared and want to protect themselves. This means they're more likely to scratch or bite, which is another reason you shouldn't try to pick up an injured animal yourself.

Note: If the county you live in doesn't have a wildlife rehabilitator on staff, search for one in a county nearby.

This Dark-Eyed Junco was trapped in a garage and released unharmed.

Have you ever encountered an injured animal? What happened to it? Were you able to help it? Write your story here.

_____

_____

_____

_____

_____

_____

_____

_____

_____

_____

_____

_____

_____

_____

_____

_____

_____

ASSEMBLING A COLLECTION OF STATE MINERALS & GEMS

As with state birds or state flowers, most states in the Northwest have state gems or minerals, but you may not have heard or know about all of them. Still, state rocks and minerals are almost always selected for their long history in the state and economic impact or for their beauty, or both. Better yet, many of these state gems, minerals, and fossils are easy to collect!

Important Note: Before you go out collecting, make sure that collecting is allowed where you're looking for rocks. Don't go onto private property when collecting, because that's against the law. In many cases, there are public places where you can legally collect rocks, though it might take some homework first!

Bring along a small container to put your collection in. This way you can collect some rocks and minerals, but not so many that you'll hurt the ecosystem or be unable to carry them home.

Finally, remember that rocks and minerals you find yourself most likely won't be polished, sparkly, and shiny like gems in a store.

QUICK DEFINITION

It can help to think of rocks and minerals like a recipe. Much like baking ingredients (say, flour and chocolate chips) go into making cookies, minerals go into making rocks. Sometimes the rocks even get cooked! **Minerals** are the ingredients for making rocks. A **rock** is made up of at least two minerals.

Minerals occur naturally—they're not made by humans. They're also inorganic—they've never been alive, and they're not made from plants or animals. Minerals are solids and have a crystal structure. They also have a definite chemical composition—each mineral is made of a particular mix of chemical elements. Sometimes, a single **chemical element** (like gold or silver) can be found in nature; those are considered minerals too.

Quartz, for example, is a mineral made of two elements: silicon and oxygen. When quartz is combined with another mineral called feldspar (and a few other mineral seasonings) and the whole mixture slowly cools under the earth, you end up with a rock called granite.

Pure Quartz Crystal Cluster

ASSEMBLING A COLLECTION OF STATE MINERALS & GEMS

DELAWARE

SILLIMANITE

The sillimanite found in Delaware is a brown, fibrous mineral. It looks like it's made of strings twisted together, making it look a little like wood. If it's cut just right, it can make a reflective "cat's eye" shape. Most of the state's sillimanite is found in the Brandywine Springs area, though you can get your best look at some at the **Delaware Museum of Natural History.**

BELEMNITE

Fossilized, extinct, squid-like animals with 10 tentacles (arms), belemnites had rows of tiny hooks, in addition to suckers, on each tentacle, similar to modern Humboldt squid. Unlike squid, however, they had an internal bone within their body cone. This cone is what you're likely to see if you come across a belemnite fossil, which is about the size and shape of a pencil. In Delaware, the best place to look for these fossils is in the dredge spoil piles on the north side of the Chesapeake and Delaware Canal, in **Fort DuPont State Park.** Please note that there aren't many fossils left here and that there are a few regulations regarding fossil collecting in this spot. Contact the park for more information: www.destateparks.com /history/fortdupont.

MARYLAND

PATUXENT RIVER STONE

This rock is easy enough to find in western Maryland, but it's a tricky one for many to identify properly. The red and yellow colors in Patuxent River Stone reminded people of the Maryland flag, which is one of the reasons it was chosen as the state gem.

Some sources say that Patuxent River Stone is an agate, or even fossilized dinosaur bones. It's not! Most geologists (rock scientists) say that it is quartzite. Besides, if it really were dino bones turned into agate, Pautuxent River Stone would be illegal and unethical (not a good choice) to collect because it would be so rare.

Good thing it's quartzite and easy (and ethical) to find! To find this stone, look along streambanks and riverbanks in western Maryland for pea-size, rusty-yellow rocks.

ECPHORA (*ECPHORA GARDNERAE GARDNERAE*)

The Ecphora was a small snail that inhabited the Chesapeake Bay area more than 5 million years ago, when the area was covered by a warm sea with sandy shores.

Ecphora is important because it was one of first North American fossils to be illustrated in a European scientific work, all the way back in 1770.

You *could* find Ecphora fossils at the Calvert Cliffs and near the St. Marys River, but it isn't likely. Ecphora fossils are found mostly on private property, and it's against the law to collect fossils on private property without permission. Though nearby Calvert Cliffs State Park is rich in many fossils, it's not a good site for collecting specimens of Ecphora.

ASTRODON JOHNSTONI

Astrodons were the first sauropods (giant plant-eating dinosaurs) described in North America, in 1865. The first specimens (samples) of Astrodons were found in Prince Georges County, in mud pits and open-pit mines.

What an Astrodon looked like exactly is a little bit of a mystery. Some of the bones found are from adults, and others are from young animals. Imagine if someone mixed two similar puzzles together and then took away the box!

You're not going to find any Astrodon fossils on your own. If you want to see an Astrodon skeleton, you can check out the **Maryland Science Center** in Baltimore.

ASSEMBLING A COLLECTION OF STATE MINERALS & GEMS

PENNSYLVANIA

Pennsylvania doesn't have a state rock, gem, fossil, or mineral. Maybe you and your classmates could work together to encourage the state government to pick one!

NEW JERSEY

HADROSAURUS FOULKII

This is it! The first discovery of its kind! The dinosaur that started it all!

Hadrosaurus foulkii was the first nearly complete dinosaur skeleton to be uncovered in the whole world, and it was found in New Jersey. The bones startled scientists: they were shaped like the bones of a reptile or a bird, but they were larger than an elephant. The bones were put on display in a museum. Imagine being one of the first people to stand next to and look up at a dinosaur skeleton!

A marl-pit miner in Haddonfield, New Jersey, uncovered some bones in the mine where he worked. A scientist named William Parker Foulke heard about his discovery and investigated further. After a summer of hard work in the slippery clay soil, the scientist's team uncovered a nearly complete *Hadrosaurus foulkii* skeleton.

You can visit the site of the original excavation in Haddonfield, although the bones have been moved into a museum. Artists and scientists made a cast (an exact molded sculpture) of the original fossil bones, because they were worried that the ancient, fragile bones would break. You can see the cast sculpture and lots of other interesting dino skeletons at the **Academy of Natural Sciences of Drexel University** in Philadelphia.

NEW YORK, CONNECTICUT & VERMONT

GARNET & GROSSULAR GARNET

If you were born in January, garnet is your birthstone. Garnets come in nearly a whole rainbow of colors, and red is the most common. They differ in color because of slight changes in their chemical components (ingredients).

The cracked surfaces of industrial-grade New York garnets prevent them from being valued as gemstones, but they are still very useful! New York garnets are some of the hardest in the world. Factories grind up the garnet and turn it into all kinds of abrasive (rough) materials, from sandpaper to glass-polishing equipment. **Barton Mines,** in New York's Adirondack Mountains, is famous for its garnets and is the oldest family-owned mine in the United States.

If you'd like to hunt for garnets on a guided tour, you can do that at the Barton Mines. To find garnets on your own, check out the abandoned **Hooper Mine,** an overgrown quarry (a type of mine) on New York State land. To get to the mine, the best place to park is at Garnet Hill Lodge, a nearby hotel. The lodge owners allow this, and it's always polite to stop by their front desk to let them know you're using the trails.

Connecticut's garnets are almandine garnets, which shine a deeper purplish red than garnets from New York. If you'd like to look for garnets in Connecticut, check out the **Connecticut Garnet Trail,** designed by the state Department of Energy and Environmental Protection.

Vermont's grossular garnets range from reddish brown to olive green to yellow, with reddish brown being the most common color. Grossular garnets are exceptionally transparent (see-through) and have large crystals. Because they're softer than other kinds of garnets, they're best suited for making jewelry. The word *grossular* comes from *Grossularia,* a scientific name for gooseberries. (A kind of grossular garnet found in Siberia is a shade of green like the color of gooseberries.)

To find garnets in Vermont, consider joining a rock and mineral club, which might be able to help you find safe places to look for them.

ASSEMBLING A COLLECTION OF STATE MINERALS & GEMS

NEW YORK

EURYPTERUS REMIPES (SEA SCORPION)

Eurypterus remipes is the scientific name of an extinct animal often referred to as a sea scorpion, which lived more than 400 million years ago in the ancient tropical seas covering New York. The sea scorpion and fossils like it are very rare worldwide, and New York State is one of only a few places in the whole world where they are commonly found.

You're unlikely to find a sea scorpion fossil on your own; they're best discovered by breaking rocks apart with a heavy chisel. (And it would be unethical to take the last of something so rare!)

If you're interested in finding other cool fossils, check out upstate New York. Many streambanks near Buffalo and Lake Erie have crumbled rocks with exposed fossils.

CONNECTICUT

EUBRONTES (THREE-TOED DINOSAUR)

The Connecticut Valley is one of the best places in the world to see all kinds of dinosaur tracks, including the tracks from a dinosaur called Eubrontes. The dinosaurs who made these large, three-toed tracks lived around 200 million years ago and stomped around in the mud near a shallow sea. Eventually, these muddy footprints turned to sedimentary rock. Even though no fossils from the dinosaur that made the tracks have been found, the tracks' size, shape, and walking pattern signal that the animal walked on its hind legs and is probably related to a dinosaur called the Dilophosaurus.

When state workers were clearing an area in Rocky Hill in the late 1960s, they made an astonishing discovery: dinosaur tracks! Stopping their construction project, scientists uncovered over 2,000 Eubrontes tracks.

The State of Connecticut created **Dinosaur State Park** to preserve the tracks and teach people more about them. You can visit the park to see the tracks for yourself.

MASSACHUSETTS

ROXBURY PUDDINGSTONE

Roxbury puddingstone is a **conglomerate,** or a bunch of different types of rocks naturally stuck together. You can see the round individual rocks in puddingstone, inside what looks like concrete holding it all together. (Roxbury is a neighborhood in Boston where much of this rock is found.)

More than 500 million years ago, wind and rain broke down large rocks and washed them down rivers. Before the smaller, tumbled rocks could break down further, mud and other sediment covered them up. Over a long period of time, the mixed-up sediment and rocks hardened into puddingstone.

Puddingstone was a very popular building material in the late 1800s, becoming more popular than red brick in the Boston area. Many Boston churches and public buildings are constructed of puddingstone.

Puddingstone looks sort of like an older style of a dessert you might know: pudding! Years ago, some cooks put pieces of fruit in their pudding, just like there are small pieces of rocks in the puddingstone.

RHODONITE

Named after *rhodon,* the Greek word for "rose," rhodonite is pink! It can be anywhere from dark pink to pale pink and even brownish. Many rhodonite pieces have black manganese streaks running through them. The rosy-pink variety of rhodonite is prized by jewelry makers.

A mine near Plainfield, Massachusetts, is the only spot in the state to find rhodonite. Since the mine is on private property, you'll need to look for samples of rhodonite online or in a gift shop—and that can be expensive.

BABINGTONITE

Babingtonite forms small, black, wedge-shaped crystals in an **igneous,** or volcanic, rock. Mineral collectors and mineralogists collect babingtonite, although it's not used much by jewelry makers or in factories.

Massachusetts is one of the few places in the world to find babingtonite. Most of the places to find it are in old quarries and mines, where machines have dug deep into the earth. You might be able to find some along road cuts near Westfield.

Massachusetts continued on next page

MASSACHUSETTS (*CONTINUED*)

DINOSAUR TRACKS

Many kinds of dinosaur tracks are common in the Northeast. The same ancient sea that extended into Connecticut 200 million years ago was in Massachusetts, too, and it was perfect for making dinosaur tracks.

In 1802, farmer Pliny Moody was plowing his field when he turned over a large rock that happened to have tracks on the back. At the time, dinosaurs weren't even known to exist! It took several decades of study before scientists decided the tracks Moody found were dinosaur tracks.

If you'd like to see some dinosaur tracks for yourself, you're in luck! From April to the end of November, you can visit **Dinosaur Footprints,** a wilderness reservation in Holyoke, Massachusetts. (It's closed in winter due to icy, slippery conditions). Allow a minimum of half an hour for your adventure, and wear good walking shoes. If you'd rather see footprints in a museum, you can visit the **Beneski Museum of Natural History** at Amherst College. Admission is free.

RHODE ISLAND

CUMBERLANDITE

Cumberlandite is an **igneous** (volcanic) rock only found in Rhode Island's Blackstone Valley and a few points south.

Cumberlandite is brownish black with white crystals, and it's really heavy for its size. It will sometimes stick to a magnet because it contains so much iron.

To find cumberlandite, you can go on a hike in Cumberland, Rhode Island. It's in the woods on a dirt trail, behind a cemetery. Park on the side of the road by the Ballou Cemetery, and follow the dirt trail leading around the cemetery. The trail will lead you to big cumberlandite outcroppings in about ¼ mile. You can also see cumberlandite samples at **Roger Williams Park Museum of Natural History and Planetarium** in Providence.

BOWENITE

Bowenite ranges in color from yellow to green to bluish gray. Bowenite is too brittle (breakable) to be used much in jewelry in the U.S. On the other side of the world, in New Zealand, the native Māori people use bowenite for both jewelry and tools.

Bowenite is most common in northern Rhode Island. The places it's found are on private property, so look for bowenite online or in a gift shop.

VERMONT

GRANITE, MARBLE & SLATE

Vermont has three state rocks!

Granite is an **igneous rock** formed from liquid magma deep underground. Extreme pressures and a slow cooling process bake granite into one of the hardest and densest rocks on the planet. The granite from Barre, Vermont, is world-famous as a stone for statues and buildings. You can take a tour of a granite quarry at **Rock of Ages** near Barre.

Marble is a **metamorphic rock**, or a rock that has changed from being cooked and/or pressurized. The marble quarry in Danby, Vermont, is the world's largest underground quarry. Vermont marble ranges in color from pure white to black. Vermont marble has many uses, including as a building material and as crushed stone that's used as an ingredient in making paint, paper, and plastic.

Slate is also a **metamorphic rock**, formed by the compacting (intense squishing) and heating of clay. Slate splits into thin slabs and is used to make roofing shingles, sidewalks, and floor tiles. The Vermont Department of Tourism created a road trip map called the **Vermont Stone Trail,** with stops at quarries, buildings made of Vermont stones, and landmarks. The Vermont Stone Trail covers much of the state. It could be fun to visit some important Vermont rock spots with your family!

TALC

Vermont talc is used in many manufactured products, including paints, plastics, and in talcum powder (used to make baby powder). Found in southwestern Vermont, mineral talc is light green and very soft.

Vermont used to be a major supplier of talc, but that stopped because of health and safety concerns. Talc forms right next to another mineral—asbestos—that can give people cancer if they breathe in its dust.

Vermont continued on next page

VERMONT (*CONTINUED*)

THE CHARLOTTE WHALE

Workers building a railroad in western Vermont uncovered a fossilized Beluga Whale skeleton. This skeleton was found near the town of Charlotte, Vermont, so it became known as the Charlotte Whale.

Designated as Vermont's state marine fossil in 2014, the Charlotte Whale is about 12,500 years old and is the same species of Beluga Whale that lives in our oceans today. You can visit the Charlotte Whale at the **Perkins Museum of Geology** in Burlington.

MOUNT HOLLY MAMMOTH TOOTH & TUSK

Railroad workers in Mount Holly, Vermont, uncovered a huge tooth and tusk, which scientists later decided came from a mammoth. Woolly mammoths lived in Vermont at the end of the last ice age, around 10,000 years ago.

You can see the Mount Holly Mammoth Tooth and Tusk at the **Mount Holly Community Historical Museum** in Belmont Village. The tooth and tusk were named Vermont's state terrestrial fossil in 2014.

NEW HAMPSHIRE

GRANITE

New Hampshire's nickname is "The Granite State." About half of the bedrock of New Hampshire is made of granite. Granite is an igneous rock formed from liquid magma deep underground. Extreme pressures and a slow cooling process bake granite into one of the hardest and densest rocks on the planet.

New Hampshire granite is famous as a building material. The original Library of Congress building in Washington, D.C., officially known as the Thomas Jefferson Building, is made of New Hampshire granite.

New Hampshire used to have a famous natural mountain landmark called Old Man of the Mountain: five ledges on a granite cliff that together looked like an old man's face. Unfortunately, the Old Man crumbled in 2003, but you can see what's left of him at **Profile Plaza** on Interstate 93.

BERYL

Worldwide, beryl is an important product. It is used as a gemstone and in many electronic devices. The chemical element beryllium, which is obtained from beryl, is used in cell phones and batteries. Adding beryllium makes the electronic parts stronger and more flexible.

The beryl found in New Hampshire is yellowish but isn't used as a gemstone. New Hampshire's beryl was mined for its use in nuclear weapons, and it was heavily guarded. (Beryl has to be treated by and added to chemicals in a certain way to make the weapons. It isn't going to explode under the ground or in your phone or tablet.)

Ever changed the battery in the remote control for your TV? The little springy thing next to where the batteries go is made with beryllium. You don't even have to go rock hunting for this one!

SMOKY QUARTZ

Smoky Quartz Is found in granite. The clear yet darkened crystals can get pretty large (and too big to fit in your pocket). Occasionally, people make jewelry out of Smoky Quartz.

The easiest way to find Smoky Quartz is to buy it online or at a gift shop. If you're up for a quartz-finding adventure, you can visit the nationally recognized **Moat Mountain Mineral Site,** near Conway, New Hampshire. Visiting the site involves driving on a gravel road and hiking in areas with few trails (or bathrooms). Collecting is only available seasonally.

MAINE

TOURMALINE

Maine has beautiful tourmaline, valued by jewelers and collectors worldwide. Maine tourmaline comes in various colors, ranging from pink to bluish green. The first major tourmaline discovery in Maine occurred in 1820 at Mount Mica in Paris, Maine, by two teenagers who were exploring the countryside.

Maine tourmaline crystals are huge! One tourmaline crystal was so big (10 inches long) that it was nicknamed the "Jolly Green Giant"; it's now in the Smithsonian National Museum of Natural History in Washington, D.C.

You can see samples of tourmaline at the **Maine Mineral & Gem Museum** in Bethel, Maine. There are also several tourist shops that let you dig through mined gravel for gems. If you're up for a self-guided tourmaline-finding adventure, you can visit **Mount Apatite,** near Auburn, Maine. Visiting the site involves hiking uphill in some areas.

Maine continued on next page

ASSEMBLING A COLLECTION OF STATE MINERALS & GEMS

MAINE (*CONTINUED*)

PERTICA QUADRIFOLIA

Pertica quadrifolia is the scientific name of a plant fossil that is found only in Maine and a few other places in the world. Plant fossils are so rare because plants' soft tissues often rot before they turn to stone, unlike hard, sturdy dinosaur bones.

This 6-foot-tall plant lived about 390 million years ago, in what's now Baxter State Park near Mount Katahdin. It was one of the tallest plants alive during the time period. Like all plants at the time, *Pertica* didn't have any leaves. Instead, it was shaped kind of like a toilet brush: it had a strong center stalk with lots of forked branches coming off.

You can see Maine *Pertica quadrifolia* fossils at the **L. C. Bates Museum** in Hinckley, Maine.

Please be aware that it is illegal to remove fossils or minerals from Baxter State Park. Fossil specimens should be left where they are found for other park users to enjoy and learn from.

QUICK QUIZ

Which of the below materials are fossils?

A. Granite

B. Belemnite

C. Garnet

D. Cumberlandite

E. *Hadrosaurus foulkii*

Answer on page 158!

SAND SLEUTH

You might think all sand is the same: light tan in color, fluffy, and not all that interesting. But take a closer look—there's more to sand than you might think.

WHAT YOU'LL NEED

- Sand (sand of any kind works for this; you can even try sand from different areas)
- Containers for your sand
- Black paper
- Magnifying glass
- **Optional:** a magnet and some vinegar

WHAT TO DO

The next time you're at a beach, collect a few small samples of sand in a jar or zip-top plastic bag. Then bring your sand home for this experiment. To keep your workspace neater, you can do this experiment on an old baking sheet.

Sprinkle some sand on the black paper, thinly enough that you can see individual grains of sand. Look at each tiny grain through the magnifying glass. What do you notice? Colors? Sizes? Try it again using sand from a different spot. Compare your observations.

Optional: Drag a magnet through the sand. If any grains stick to the magnet, that means the sand contains a lot of iron.

Put a drop of vinegar on the sand. If it fizzes, that means your sand contains bones or shells. (Be sure to wash your hands after using vinegar.)

TESTING THE HARDNESS OF MINERALS

Hardness is a useful way to help identify your mineral finds. The **Mohs Hardness Scale**, on the right, ranks some common minerals in terms of hardness, or how easily they can be scratched. Talc, the lowest mineral on the scale, is so soft you can scratch it with your fingers. Diamond is famous for being one of the hardest minerals, and for good reason: almost no natural substances can scratch it.

Making your own hardness test kit is a good way to start learning hands-on with rocks and minerals. Determining a mineral's hardness is a good first step in trying to identify it.

The way the scale works is simple: any material lower on the scale can be scratched by materials above it. So gypsum can scratch talc, but talc can't scratch gypsum. Similarly, calcite, which is a 3, can scratch gypsum *and* talc.

WHAT YOU'LL NEED

Using the scale to test your finds usually goes like this: You find a mineral (not a rock!) and you're not sure what it is. You start out by trying to scratch it with your fingernail. If it leaves a scratch, then it's softer than 2.5 on the scale. Chances are, however, it won't leave a scratch. So you need to move up to a different piece of equipment with a known hardness.

Here are some common, easy-to-find examples:

• Fingernail: 2.5

• A real piece of copper (not a penny, as these coins aren't made of much copper anymore): 3

• Steel nail or a knife: 5.5–6 (for safety reasons, you should have an adult help you with these tests)

• A piece of quartz: 7

Talc
$Mg_3Si_4O_{10}(OH)_2$

Gypsum
$CaSO_4 \cdot 2H_2O$

Calcite
$CaCO_3$

Fluorite
CaF_2

Apatite
$Ca_5(PO_4)_3(F,Cl,OH)$

WHAT TO DO

To scratch it, you need to hold the to-be-scratched mineral firmly in one hand, and use a pointed area of the "scratching" mineral and press firmly, away from your body or fingers. If it leaves a scratch mark, it's softer than the "scratching" mineral. Obviously, for safety reasons you should make sure you have an adult conduct the actual scratch tests—don't handle a knife or a nail yourself.

Once you've found something that scratches it, you're pretty close to figuring out its hardness. Then it's just a matter of scratching it with other minerals from the chart or your scratching tools, then seeing if you can figure out an even more specific range. Once you've narrowed down the hardness some more, looking up mineral hardness is easy online.

Note: You can also buy lab-calibrated "hardness pick" kits; these are much more accurate, but they can be expensive.

Keep track of your hardness tests here. Doing so can help you learn to identify your finds!

6

Orthoclase
$KAlSi_3O_8$

7

Quartz
SiO_2

8

Topaz
$Al_2SiO_4(F,OH)_2$

9

Corundum
Al_2O_3

10

Diamond
C

MAKE A CAST OF AN ANIMAL TRACK

You might think that animal tracks don't last very long, but that isn't always true. Remember the dinosaurs that left the tracks in the Connecticut River Valley? Follow the instructions below to make your very own track cast!

WHAT YOU'LL NEED

- A ring of plastic larger than your track. (Cutting a ring off the top of a margarine or yogurt container works great.)

- Plaster of Paris

- A container for mixing and a spoon to mix with

WHAT TO DO

Have an adult help you when creating a cast—this can get a bit tricky.

1. Remove any twigs or leaves around the track.

2. Use the plastic to create a "wall" around the track.

3. Make the plaster. Add two parts plaster for every one part water (so if you use 1 cup of plaster, you should use $1/2$ cup of water). Mix until the plaster isn't lumpy, usually at least a few minutes.

4. Pour the plaster inside your wall (but not directly onto the track), letting the plaster flow over the track gradually. Make sure you pour enough to cover the entire track to a depth of about $3/4$ inch.

5. Wait half an hour, then test the firmness of the plaster. Once it's hard enough, remove it by grabbing it at the edges. Wait a few days for it to dry completely.

MAKE A SELF-PORTRAIT USING NATURE

WHAT YOU'LL NEED

• Several blank pieces of paper—could be computer paper, a paper bag, anything!

• A glue stick, if you want to create a permanent piece of art

WHAT TO DO

With an adult, start out by gathering some twigs; these are a great way to create a general outline of your face. Then start thinking about the color of your skin, hair, and eyes, and look around for natural objects that are a close match. It's best to choose from things that you know are safe to touch: rocks and pebbles, sand, dandelions, flower petals, oaks, maples, grass, moss, tree bark, and so on. If you're not sure about touching something, leave it alone or check with an adult. That way, you can avoid Poison Ivy, Poison Oak, Poison Sumac, and anything else you shouldn't be touching.

When you're done, take a picture of your portrait; then put your natural parts back where you found them, and put your paper in the recycling or trash. You can also glue each object to the paper and then frame it. Just make sure that no little kids have access to the actual leaves and flowers and such. (Little kids often like to touch and lick and eat lots of things they shouldn't.)

GEOLOGY & GEMSTONES CROSSWORD

ACROSS

5. Used to make baby powder, but not as much anymore. Don't breathe in the dust!

6. This rock is found only in Rhode Island. It's slightly magnetic and really heavy.

8. The first dinosaur uncovered in North America.

9. This is a general name for a rock that has been changed under intense heat and/or pressure from underground.

10. This Maine gem forms large crystals, and it even has a "watermelon" type.

13. A giant sauropod that is the state dinosaur of Maryland.

DOWN

1. Dinosaurs walking through ancient seas made these.

2. A Massachusetts rock that's a bunch of different rocks stuck together.

3. Several states have this as their official mineral or gemstone. It's used to make sandpaper rough and is usually reddish if cut into a gemstone.

4. The chemical element beryllium is used in electrical parts; it's found in this mineral with a similar name.

7. This New Hampshire and Vermont building material is used for everything from sculptures to buildings.

11. This is a classic building and sculpting material. It's a metamorphic rock.

12. Another word for *volcanic*.

Answers on page 159!

New Hampshire's Old Man of the Mountain after its "face" mostly collapsed

LEARNING TO IDENTIFY BASIC GROUPS OF BUGS

Scientists group the creatures they study into different categories based on many different things: body type, kinds of or lack of wings, habitat, and more. Deciding what critter goes where is called **classification.** You'll notice a word in parentheses **( )** after the bug names in capital letters below—this is the **order** (a type of scientific name) for each group. All of the animals discussed here are **invertebrates,** or animals without a backbone.

BUTTERFLIES & MOTHS (LEPIDOPTERA)

White-Lined Sphinx Moth

Cecropia Moth Caterpillar

Cecropia Moth

Rosy Maple Moth

Monarch Butterfly

Viceroy Butterfly

Eastern Tiger Swallowtail

Pearl Crescent

FLIES (DIPTERA)

House Fly

Robber Fly

Mosquito

Margined Calligrapher Fly

BEETLES (COLEOPTERA)

Potato Beetle

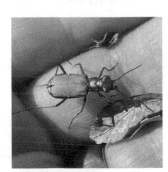

Six-Spotted Tiger Beetle

Carrion Beetle

Goldenrod Soldier Beetle

Broad-Necked Root Borer

Green June Beetle

Red Milkweed Beetle

Common Eastern Firefly

LEARNING TO IDENTIFY BASIC GROUPS OF BUGS

ANTS, BEES & WASPS (HYMENOPTERA)

Honeybee

Bumblebee

Yellow Jacket

Giant Ichneumon Wasp

Eastern Carpenter Bee

Bald-Faced Hornet

Carpenter Ant

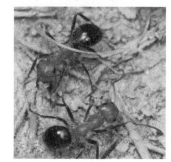

Allegheny Mound Ant

DAMSELFLIES & DRAGONFLIES (ODONATA)

Springtime Darner

Painted Skimmer

Ebony Jewelwing

Powdered Dancer

GRASSHOPPERS & RELATIVES (ORTHOPTERA)

Grasshopper

Cricket

Northern
Bush Katydid

Greenhouse
Camel Cricket

TRUE BUGS (HEMIPTERA)

Dog-Day Cicada

Leafhopper

Stink Bug

Treehopper

OTHER FRESHWATER INSECTS (EPHEMEROPTERA, TRICHOPTERA, PLECOPTERA)

Giant Mayfly

Speckled Dun

Caddisfly

Stonefly

LEARNING TO IDENTIFY
BASIC GROUPS OF BUGS

SPIDERS

Orb-Weaver
Spider

Cobweb Spider

Goldenrod
Crab Spider

Bronze
Jumping Spider

OTHER BUG-LIKE CREATURES

Isopod (Roly Poly,
Pill Bug)

Centipede

Millipede

Worm

QUICK QUIZ

Which of these are insects?

A. Dog-Day Cicada   B. Painted   C. Orb-Weaver
                      Skimmer   Spider

D. Monarch   E. Isopod (Roly
    Butterfly   Poly, Pill Bug)

Answers on page 158!

RAISE NATIVE CATERPILLARS & RELEASE THEM

Finding a caterpillar is one of the highlights of spring and summer. But unless it's a really well-known caterpillar, like a Monarch, identifying caterpillars can be tricky for beginners. Many caterpillars, including all of the classic inchworms, will actually end up being moths.

But you don't need to identify your caterpillar to rear it; after all, one of the most fun ways to identify a moth or a butterfly is after it's turned into an adult!

Note: It's best to collect only smooth or slightly bumpy caterpillars and leave the fuzzy ones alone. Caterpillars with fuzz or hairs may make you itch if you touch them.

WHAT YOU'LL NEED

- A butterfly house (it's best to purchase a high-quality one online first)

- An ample supply of fresh leaves (use the ones you found your caterpillar on, and some from plants near that spot)

- A water source for the leaves, but one that the caterpillar can't enter (pill bottles work great)

WHAT TO DO

First, set up your butterfly house; this way, it's ready to go once you catch your caterpillar. Many common commercially available butterfly houses are mesh cylinders.

The next thing you need to do is prepare your water source for the host plants (the plants your caterpillar needs to eat to become an adult). Do not put a water dish or another water source at the bottom of a butterfly house; caterpillars drown easily. Instead, have a parent help you drill or cut a hole in a small container like an old pill bottle, and put the plant stems into the water source—but make sure the caterpillar can't fall into the water and drown.

Now go outside and track down a caterpillar! When you find one, immediately note what plant you find it on or, if it's on

the ground, the plants that are nearby. These are likely the caterpillar's host plants. If you're unsure of which plants to gather, bring in a sampling of several different kinds. If you want an exact answer, post a photo of your caterpillar on a site like BugGuide.net or iNaturalist, and ask for help in finding out what it eats.

Put your caterpillar, along with its host plants, in your butterfly house. Remember to put your plants in the water container. You'll need to replace the leaves every few days, as well as clean up the caterpillar's poop (known as frass). Eventually, the caterpillar will begin to pupate. And if all goes well, it will come out of its chrysalis, or cocoon, as a butterfly or a moth!

If you're worried about your caterpillar, keep these tips in mind:

Keep your caterpillar container clean—if it's dirty, your caterpillar might get sick. If you find a caterpillar in late summer, it might be one that spends the winter as a pupa and thus takes longer than you expect to turn into an adult. Finally, parasitic wasps often lay eggs inside caterpillars. Unfortunately, it's hard to tell if your caterpillar has parasites, and there's not much you can do if they hatch. (Parasites are creatures that feed on other organisms while they're still alive.)

Still, with practice, there's a good chance that you'll get to watch moths and butterflies all summer! A tip for capturing caterpillars: pick up the whole leaf that it's on; don't worry about scooping up the caterpillar separately. Caterpillars are easy to squish by accident if you try to pick them up; using a leaf to carry them is a better option.

GET TO KNOW THE NORTHEAST'S NATIVE BEES

If you've been following the news, you know that bee populations are in trouble. But you're probably most familiar with honeybees, which are actually an introduced species that is originally from Europe, not the U.S. Think of honeybees as farm animals—the honeybees you see in your yard are, in a sense, kind of like escaped chickens or cows.

Domesticated honeybee populations have run into trouble over the past few decades due to a combination of factors, including pests (especially the Varroa mite), pesticide use, and habitat loss. These domesticated insects play a critical role in pollinating agricultural crops, especially almonds, blueberries, and cherries.

Honeybees aren't the only bees in the U.S. that are threatened. On the contrary, while honeybees get much of the press, thousands of other native bee species in the U.S. are in trouble too! Many of them are threatened or in danger due to loss of food and nesting materials, pesticides, parasites and diseases, climate change, the introduction of nonnative species to new regions, and combinations of all of these things.

Native bees in the Northeast range from the familiar fuzzy bumblebees that flutter among your flowers to tiny squash bees that feed on squash blossoms. In fact, there are about 440 species (kinds) of bees in the state of Pennsylvania alone.

BEES

Bumblebees
Fuzzy all over, black and yellow, bumblebees nest underground.

Carpenter Bees
Fuzzy only on the head and thorax (midsection). Abdomen (tail end) is shiny black. Chews holes in wood to make nests.

Rusty-Patched Bumblebee
Endangered species. Few have been found in the Northeast. Worker bees and males have a rusty-reddish patch on their backs.

Sweat Bees
Some species of Sweat Bees are attracted to the smell of human sweat. They nest in the ground.

Mining Bees
Mining Bees get their name because they nest in the ground in sandy soil.

Leaf-Cutter Bees
Leaf-Cutter Bees line their nests with leaf pieces.

Mason Bees
These bees nest in already-existing holes in cracks in stone or wood, and they line the nest holes with mud.

Squash Bees
Squash Bees live almost entirely on nectar and pollen from squash and pumpkin flowers. They nest in the ground near squash plants.

BEE LOOK-ALIKES & BEETLES

The insects below only look like bees—they're actually flies or beetles. Why might an insect try to **mimic**, or copy, a bee?

Flower Flies/ Hoverflies
Hoverflies get their name from their tendency to hover over flowers.

Bee Flies
They're fuzzy like a bumblebee!

Ornate Snipe Fly
This fly lives in and near forests.

Locust Borer
This beetle has zigzag stripes, unlike a bee's straight stripes. Locust Borer larvae feed on locust trees.

QUICK QUIZ

Which one of these is a bee?

1.

2.

3.

Answers on page 158!

START AN INSECT COLLECTION

If you love bugs, creating a bug collection can help you observe them up close, but if you're not into killing bugs, there's another option. When you're out in nature, chances are you'll notice dead insects if you're paying attention. If a bug is dead but in reasonably good shape, you can add it to your collection. You'll be surprised at what you find: butterflies and moths, gorgeous beetles, and so on. (After all, insects don't live very long.)

One of the easiest ways to store insects is with a Riker Mount, a simple glass case with padding that holds the insects against the glass.

OPTIONAL PROJECT

If you want to collect live samples, placing them in a zip-top plastic bag and freezing them is one way to kill them humanely. On sites like BugGuide.net, you can also look up "killing jars" online that use common household chemicals.

What is your favorite type of insect? Why?

_____

_____

_____

MAKE AN ULTRAVIOLET BUG TRAP

Have you ever noticed how bugs are attracted to lights at night? This happens because nocturnal insects use light to navigate, and artificial lights confuse them. With a simple setup, you can make your own "light trap" to attract bugs. It's a wonderful way to see insects that you might not see otherwise.

WHAT YOU'LL NEED

- A lantern, an ultraviolet lamp, or a blacklight (available online)
- An extension cord
- An old bedsheet or a curtain (a light-colored one is best)
- Two sections of rope
- A pair of scissors
- Flashlights
- A camera

WHAT TO DO

With an adult supervising, cut holes in the corners at one end of the bedsheet, and have the adult help you tie a section of rope to each hole in the bedsheet or curtain. (Curtains often have ready-made loops that make things easier.)

Then look for a good spot to find bugs; generally, the wilder it is, the better, but you'll need to be within reach of an outdoor-safe extension cord so you can plug in your light. Near woods, bushes, or other plants is good, but even the middle of a suburban yard will have all sorts of bugs you've likely never seen.

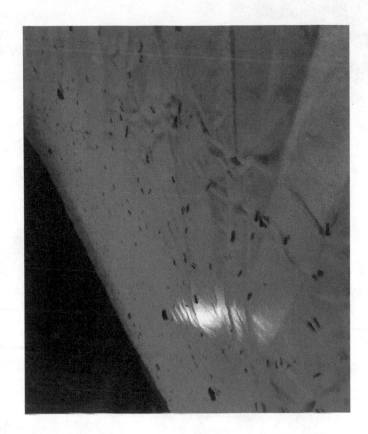

Once you get a look at the insects you've attracted, wait a while longer, and visit again later in the night (some of the best bug hunting is late at night).

Note: When you're observing moths, the light might shine on you and your clothes a bit, so it's possible (though not all that likely) to have moths or other bugs land on you. To avoid this, wear a dark shirt (not one that matches the "moth sheet"). A few bugs may land on you anyway, but gently brushing them off with a stick or a gloved hand is enough to make them fly away.

Tie one end of the rope to a support, such as a tree branch, bird feeder hook, or fence post. Then drag the other rope on the other side of the sheet or curtain until the whole thing is taut and hanging like a movie screen. Tie the bottom to a chair or anything else that's heavy enough to hold it, or put heavy rocks on the bottom. About an hour before sunset, find a chair and place it in front of or behind the sheet. Put your lantern or UV lamp on the chair, and point it so the light shines onto the curtain. If your light doesn't use batteries, plug it into an outdoor-safe extension cord.

Then it's time to wait. Make periodic visits to the sheet to see what you find! Heading out with a flashlight in one hand and a camera in another is an easy way to record your finds (and then identify them later).

CRICKET MATH

Crickets are famously noisy insects; the males rub their front wings (not their legs!) together to attract females. That much you probably knew. But did you know that you can count a cricket's chirps to tell the approximate temperature outside?

The math is simple: Go outside and listen for a cricket that's chirping. Count the number of its chirps for 13 seconds, then add 40 to that total. Then check it against the temperature for your area: go to www.noaa.gov and find your local weather in the top-right corner.

Pretty wild, right? Try it again on a different day and record your findings below.

The reason this works out is actually relatively simple: Crickets, like all insects, are cold-blooded, so their body temperature depends on the surrounding air. So when it's warmer, their metabolism speeds up, and so do the chirps! When it's colder, their chirps slow down.

Number of chirps in 13 seconds _____ + 40 = _____

Number of chirps in 13 seconds _____ + 40 = _____

Number of chirps in 13 seconds _____ + 40 = _____

Number of chirps in 13 seconds _____ + 40 = _____

Number of chirps in 13 seconds _____ + 40 = _____

Number of chirps in 13 seconds _____ + 40 = _____

[1] Original research via Dr. Peggy LeMone and James Larsen. https://www.questia.com/library/journal/1G1-272666064/the-sound-of-crickets-using-evidence-based-reasoning

BUGS & INSECTS CROSSWORD

ACROSS

1. This insect is very important for many farmers, as it helps pollinate their crops, but it's not native to North America.

4. The word for the wiggly larvae (juveniles) of moths or butterflies.

7. Butterflies usually fly during the day; this group of related insects look similar, but most (but not all) fly at night.

9. This animal isn't an insect at all; robins love to eat them.

Answers on page 159!

DOWN

2. This group of insects has a hard outer covering on their wings. Ladybugs and June bugs belong to this group.

3. This insect is famous for chirping at night, and by counting its chirps for 13 seconds, you can even use it as a thermometer!

5. These beautiful, fast-flying insects zoom through the summer air, snatching bugs in midair. They land with their wings spread open.

6. This group of caterpillars is known to scientists as the geometers, but most people call them this, for how they seem to "measure out" distance as they walk along.

8. This group of non-insects has eight legs and two body sections.

LOOKING AT SOIL, DIRT, OR A DEAD LOG

Rocks and minerals are definitely showier than plain old dirt or soil, but that's only until you get an up-close look. Once you do, with a magnifying glass, a macro camera, or a small microscope, you'll be surprised at what you find.

WHAT TO DO

Roll over a dead log and strip off a piece of bark. A dead log might look, well, dead, but it's actually its own little world. Insects, such as wasps, burrow into the wood to lay their eggs. Under the bark, ants and beetles are busy tunneling or making a home (they often leave behind intricate patterns on the wood). And it's easy to spot tiny mushrooms and sometimes very colorful slime molds, which are often food sources for other animals, such as slugs, snails, and insects. Once you start looking closely, it's easy to find a lot more life forms than you might expect.

Important Note: If you have venomous spiders or snakes in your area, make sure you go out with an adult and take proper precautions (wear gloves, long pants, and so on) when digging in dirt or turning over logs.

WHAT YOU MIGHT SEE

• Slugs or tiny land snails

• Lichen (an organism that consists of algae and/or bacteria and fungi, all living together)

• Slime molds

• Spiders, ants, tiny insects, and other animals

QUICK QUESTIONS

1. How many types of life did you find?

_____

_____

2. Were you able to identify them all?

_____

_____

START LOOKING AT MUSHROOMS

When you think of mushrooms, you might think of the red-and-white mushrooms from *Super Mario Brothers* or the familiar white mushrooms sold at the grocery store. There are only two types of fungi, but scientists think there may be millions of species in the world—most of which scientists don't know much (if anything) about.

The Northeast alone is probably home to thousands of fungi species. Some have a **mutualistic** (equally beneficial) relationship with trees, helping the trees get nutrients while the mushrooms get a place to live. Others are **saprobes** (which consume dead or dying trees or other natural materials). Still others are microscopic but very important, such as the yeast—yes, a fungus!— that helps make the bread in your sandwich.

In the Northeast, mushrooms can be classified in a few simple ways. Obviously, this list is not all-inclusive, and it won't replace a field guide (or five!), but these general categories are helpful to know.

No-Duh Safety Note: Do **not** eat wild mushrooms. Some are very toxic to eat and tricky to identify. Wait until you're older and have trained, experienced adults to help you out. If you want to pick up or touch a mushroom to get a closer look, wear gloves. And if you're making a spore print or sketch, do that outside. Throw the mushrooms in the garbage when you're done.

See page 124 for our tips on spotting mushrooms.

CAP & STEM WITH GILLS

Mushrooms with a stem and a cap, with gills underneath.
These mushrooms often look like an umbrella.

Red Fly Agaric
*(the "Super Mario"
mushroom)*

Laccaria
(very common)

Inky Caps

Witch's Hat

CAP & STEM WITH PORES

Mushrooms with a cap and a stem, but with tiny holes
(pores) underneath.

Birch Bolete

Bolete

King Bolete

Slippery Jack

START LOOKING AT MUSHROOMS

SHELF MUSHROOMS

Mushrooms that mostly grow out from trees, like a shelf; they can have pores or gills.

Chicken of the Woods

Artist's Conk

Shelf Fungus

Oyster Mushroom

Birch Polypore

Milk-White Toothed Polypore

Red Band Fungus

Hemlock Varnish

ROUND MUSHROOMS

Round or oval mushrooms that grow on the ground. Some puffballs can get as big as a soccer ball, but don't breathe in the dust when they "pop," because it's unhealthy.

Giant Puffball

A smaller species of puffball

Earthball

False Truffles

SURPRISING MUSHROOMS

Mushrooms that are hard to describe because of their brain-like shapes or weird consistency.

Coral Fungi

Bear's Head Tooth

Willow Brain/ Amber Jelly Fungus

Dead Man's Fingers

Morels

False Morel

Golden Chanterelle

Common Stinkhorn

START LOOKING AT MUSHROOMS

SLIME MOLDS

Slime molds were once considered fungi, but they are now classified differently. They're more like a bunch of amoebas living in a clump. Still, they are often grouped together with fungi, so here are a few! They are *weird*. In fact, they can move from one place to another (but slowly, so you need a time-lapse camera to see it), and they can complete a maze puzzle.

Dog Vomit Slime Mold (gross!)

Chocolate Tube Slime Mold

Wolf's Milk Slime

Red Raspberry Slime Mold

TIPS FOR SPOTTING MUSHROOMS

- Look for mushrooms after a rain (they can pop up quite quickly).

- Look near the bases of dying trees or on dead logs. Mushrooms often seem to be growing from the ground when they might actually be growing from wood in the soil.

- Slime molds often grow under bark.

1. Page through a field guide to mushrooms, then go and look for them in your area, especially if it has rained lately. Jot down your notes about them here!

_____

_____

_____

_____

_____

2. Sketch your mushroom finds here!

MAKE MUSHROOM SPORE PRINTS

Mushrooms reproduce via spores. Spores are too small to see individually without a microscope, but there's an easy and fun way to spot them: by making a spore print. For a number of technical reasons, spores aren't considered the same thing as a seed in a plant, but the basic idea is the same: spores help fungi reproduce. And they do that by leaving microscopic spores behind almost everywhere. Spore colors vary by species, and they can produce some neat results. To see for yourself, make a spore print.

WHAT YOU'LL NEED

- Small bowls or cups

- White paper and, if possible, some construction paper of various colors

- Different kinds of mushrooms, with cap and pores or cap and gills

WHAT TO DO

With a knife, cut off the cap of each mushroom—or take a good section of a shelf mushroom—and place it on top of a piece of paper. (The gills or pores should be facing down onto the paper.) Place a small bowl or a cup over each mushroom. Mushroom spore colors vary a lot, so it's helpful to change up the paper color; a mushroom with light-colored spores won't show up well on white paper, for instance. Wait an hour or so, remove the bowl, and throw the mushroom in the trash. Then admire the spore print left behind!

Important Note: Have an adult handle the knife, and don't make spore prints in your kitchen or another area where food is served, or where someone could mistake the mushrooms for food. A garage is a good place to make spore prints.

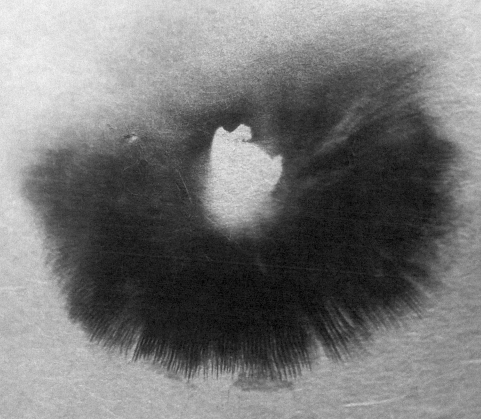

CARVE ARTIST'S CONK

Artist's Conk is a special kind of shelf mushroom that grows on dead or dying trees. At first glance, it doesn't look like much. It's pretty plain looking on the top—oval shaped and brown and white—and underneath it's just a drab white.

Artist's Conk gets its name because its white pores turn a dark brown when scratched. And the scratches then stay that way, making it a favorite of "scratch artists." This makes Artist's Conk something like nature's Etch A Sketch.

Of course, to identify Artist's Conk, you'll need an adult's help and a field guide (see page 154), but it's not too tricky to spot once you start looking.

Note: Please only carve Artist's Conk that you have collected. Don't carve it if it's still in the woods.

Before you carve your Artist's Conk, you might want to practice writing down your message here. When you write on a mushroom, you can't use an eraser, so practicing here first can help you get it right.

_____

_____

_____

_____

_____

_____

_____

_____

_____

_____

_____

_____

_____

_____

OCEANSIDE FUN

Many of the cities of the Northeast are along the coast. To get to know the ecosystems of the region, it's a good idea to check out nature at the ocean beach!

EXPLORE A TIDE POOL

A **tide pool** is an area of the shore that fills up at high tide and still holds water when the tide goes out. Tide pools are usually found among rocks but can also be found in holes in the sand or even in between tree stumps. Tide pools are their own fascinating little world. Clams filter **plankton** (microscopic plants and animals) out of the water, while small fish and crabs clean up any leftovers. You might even find sea urchins!

Safety Note 1, for you: Wear shoes with a grippy sole and a protective covering over the toes. There can be slippery, pointy rocks and sharp shells in tide pools, and you don't want to cut your feet or slip by accident.

Safety Note 2, for the creatures you discover: Remember, although tide pool creatures probably won't harm us, we can harm them if we're not careful. You'll often see more interesting behavior if you look at the tide pool creatures without disturbing them. If you do end up touching or picking up the creatures you find, pick them up gently, and fully support them in the palm of your hand. Never tug on an animal clinging to a rock or other surface. Keep animals underwater as much as possible—it helps them breathe.

Finally, please put back any rocks that you move. Do it gently, so you don't accidentally smash any of the creatures.

Take a walk along the beach, and see what you can find. If you're looking for shells, it's best to look between the **wrack line** (the line of debris left at high tide) and the water's edge. Only take a few empty shells home with you. Animals use them for shelter or nutrients, and it makes sure that everyone has a chance to see and find shells too.

Note: If you want to bring a shell home, give it a sniff first. Just say no to smelly shells—if there are pieces of decaying animal inside, the shell will stink (and will make everything near it stink too).

WHAT YOU MIGHT SEE

MOLLUSKS

These animals have a hard outer shell. Inside the shell is a soft, squishy foot that they use to move themselves along the bottom of the tide pool. Some use their body like a straw to propel themselves through the water.

UNIVALVES

These animals have one shell; *uni-* means one.

Periwinkle Snail   Knobbed Whelk   Channel Whelk   Moon Snail

GO BEACHCOMBING

BIVALVES

These animals have two shells; *bi-* means two.

Quahog

Soft-Shell Clam

Razor Clam

Oyster

Blue Mussel

Bay Scallop

Common
Jingle Shell

Ribbed Mussel

CHELICERATA (HORSESHOE CRABS)

Even though they have the word *crab* in their name,
horseshoe crabs are more closely related to spiders and
scorpions than any of the crabs on the next page.

Horseshoe Crab

CRABS

These many-legged creatures scurry around on land or swim in the water. Many are **omnivores,** meaning they eat both plants and animals.

Spider Crab

Atlantic Rock Crab

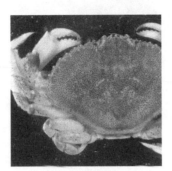
Blue Crab

Hermit Crab

Black-Fingered Rock Crab

Ghost Crab

European Green Crab

Asian Shore Crab

No-Duh Crab Note: Crabs can pinch. The smaller ones hurt less, but they can still pinch.

GO BEACHCOMBING

BARNACLES

These animals are related to crabs. The seam in the top opens up so they can filter plankton out of the water to eat.

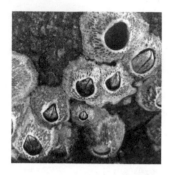  

ECHINODERMS

Echinoderm means "spiny skin." Most echinoderms can **regenerate** (regrow) hurt or damaged body parts.

Atlantic Purple Sea Urchin

Common Sea Star

Frilled Sea Anemone

SMALL FISH

The types of fish that live in tide pools stay small their whole lives, never growing longer than your index finger.

Atlantic Silverside

Mummichog

ALGAE

These organisms make their food from the sun, just like plants do on land.

Mermaid Hair Algae

Bladderwrack

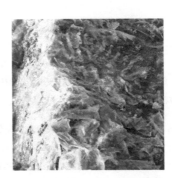

Sea Lettuce Algae

Dead Man's Fingers

SPOTTING THE MOON, THE PLANETS & ORION

In winter, it can be hard to stay active outside. After all, it's cold and it gets dark early, but for stargazers, winter is one of the best seasons around. There aren't any bugs, you don't have to stay up late for it to get really dark, and some of the best constellations are visible during the winter. So if you dress up warmly, grab a lawn chair, and bust out a small telescope or binoculars, you can see the planets, the moon, even the Orion Nebula and the Pleiades star cluster.

WHAT YOU'LL NEED

• Warm clothes

• A lawn chair

• A small telescope or, if you don't have one, binoculars

• A field guide and/or virtual planetarium software like Stellarium (which is free for Windows computers and Macs)

WHAT TO DO

First, figure out what you want to see before you head out. That's where a good field guide comes in. Virtual planetarium software is great, too, because it can show you exactly what the sky will look like wherever you are (and whenever you want).

Starting with the moon is always a good idea—it's bright and impossible to miss. when it's up. The best time to observe the moon is in its first quarter, when only one half of the moon is lit up—this reveals a lot more detail than a full moon, when all that reflected sunlight washes out the view. If you have a small telescope, try holding a smartphone over the eyepiece and see if you can snap some pictures. This can be tricky, but if you take a bunch of pictures and fiddle with the settings, you can get some wonderful shots. (There are also phone mounts you can buy fairly inexpensively online, but you have to be sure to get the right model for your phone.)

After you take a look at the moon, make sure you get a chance to see Jupiter, Saturn, Mars, and Venus. You'll need to refer to your field guide or planetarium software for when and where to look for each, because they appear to move through the sky over time. Still, it's worth the effort: seeing Saturn's rings for the first time will make you gasp.

Note: Don't expect to see the rings like you would in a picture from NASA—the planets will look pretty darn small. But if you're patient and you focus just right, you'll see the planets for real. It's an amazing experience. Even if you just have binoculars, you can often spot Jupiter's four largest moons: Io, Europa, Ganymede, and Callisto.

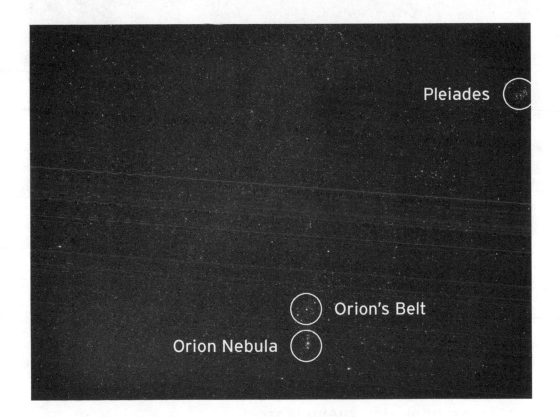

Finally, even if you only have a small telescope or binoculars, make sure to take a look at the constellation Orion. Easy to spot throughout much of the late fall and winter, it's famous for Orion's Belt, a line of three evenly spaced stars at the center of the constellation. If you look just below the belt, you'll see a star that looks a bit smudged; it's actually not a star at all. It's a **nebula,** or an area where stars are forming. Viewed through binoculars or a small telescope, it's a wonderful sight. The same is true for the Pleiades, a bright star cluster. To find it, simply follow from Orion's Belt up and to the right. If you're just looking with your eyes, it looks like a little smudge, but through binoculars or a telescope, it looks kind of like a miniature version of the Big Dipper.

Alcor

Mizar

THE BIG DIPPER'S
HIDDEN SURPRISE

Use your knowledge of the night sky, or your field guide, to find the Big Dipper. With your eyes first, find the "handle" of the dipper. Next, follow the handle up right up to where it bends, and take a look at the stars in this area. Count how many stars you see, then look again with your binoculars (or telescope). How many stars do you see this time?

These stars are Alcor (the dimmer star) and Mizar (the brighter star), also known as the Horse and Rider. In many cultures, being able to see both Alcor and Mizar was a sign of good health and good vision.

Get this, though: Alcor is really two stars spinning around each other, and Mizar is actually *four* stars spinning around each other. Then, both groups spin around each other in turn in a complex six-star system.

SPOT THE INTERNATIONAL SPACE STATION (ISS)

If you really want an amazing sight, see if you can observe the International Space Station as it passes overhead. Continuously inhabited by astronauts since the year 2000, the International Space Station is massive—longer than football field—and its huge solar panels reflect a lot of light back to Earth. This makes it incredibly bright in the night sky as it passes overhead.

WHAT TO DO

To spot it, visit the excellent website **Spot the Station** (spotthestation.nasa.gov), and check the forecast for the next times the station will pass overhead at your location. It'll be visible either in the morning (sometimes quite early) or in the evening. But if you're patient, there are quite a few options, and you can make observing the ISS a fun habit. (If you want a challenge, try snapping a photo of it as it passes overhead.)

And once you spot it, you can visit the website www.howmany peopleareinspacerightnow.com to learn who was aboard the ISS as it flew by.

1. What was it like seeing the International Space Station?

_____

_____

2. How long did you see it, and how bright was it in the sky compared to the stars and planets?

_____

_____

International Space Station

CONDUCT A BACKYARD BIO-BLITZ

A **bio-blitz** is an event where nature lovers—usually in a large group—try to record all of the life in a given area during a set period of time. For scientists and nature lovers, bio-blitzes help provide a snapshot of an area's biodiversity at any one time. But you don't need to be a scientist to do a bio-blitz; you can do one yourself or with your family. And you can do one wherever you are: in your backyard, on a trip, even from the window of a car or from an apartment balcony. The basic idea is simple: you want to try to identify as many life forms as you can within a certain amount of time.

WHAT YOU'LL NEED

- A magnifying glass
- A smartphone
- A notebook and pen for each person
- Field guides

WHAT TO DO

The simplest way to start off is in your backyard or a green space near where you live. Have an adult set a timer for 15 minutes. Start out with the easy stuff first: the grass, any weeds that you recognize (dandelions), and birds or mammals (such as chipmunks or squirrels). It's helpful to be systematic: start in one area, and look it over carefully before moving on to the next.

For each thing, write down what you think it is and where you found it. Take a picture or draw it if you don't know what it is and you want to look it up. In real bio-blitzes, there are forms for each volunteer and blanks for specific location, time, and so on, but the form on the next page (which you can also copy into your notebook) should work for yours. See how many different kinds of animals and plants you can find!

Bonus: If you can look it up, try to find the **scientific name** for what you found. Scientific names exist to make it easier for scientists to talk to each other clearly. For example, there are three main different kinds of bears in North America: Black Bears, Brown Bears, and Polar Bears. So the word *bear* isn't very specific. And for many creatures, including Insects, there simply aren't any common names. A scientific name is a special name that has two parts: a **genus name,** which is like a last name and is shared with other similar animals, and a **species name**, which is like a first name. Together, that name is unique for that animal. For example, only one plant has the name *Taraxacum officinale*: the Common Dandelion, and scientists all over the world can refer to it, even if they don't speak the same language!

Field Guide Apps: If you're interested in using a phone app to identify your mystery organisms, try **Seek** (https://www .inaturalist.org/pages/seek_app) The app is free, but please ask first before you install it on someone else's phone.

How it works: You open the app and click on the camera icon to take a photo of an animal, plant, or mushroom that you spot. The app will run the photo through a computer program that will attempt to identify it. The program isn't perfect, but it often helps you narrow down what you found. The species included in Seek are based entirely on photos and identifications made by the global iNaturalist community, which we'll go over next. All of the findings you make with Seek are private—they won't be shared publicly, making it safe for kids to use. You don't even have to create an account to use the app.

CONDUCT A BACKYARD BIO-BLITZ

Note: If you're doing this from a car window on a long drive, you obviously won't be able to take photos, but you can still note the birds, trees, roadside plants, and such that you see, along with any deer, fox, coyotes, or other critters you see along the way.

WHAT IS IT?	LOCATION	SCIENTIFIC NAME
Plants		
Dandelion	By the swing set	*Taraxacum officinale*
White Oak Tree	In the front yard	*Quercus alba*
Birds		
American Robin	On the oak tree	*Turdus migratorious*
Mammals		
Gray Squirrel	?	
Insects		
Unidentified but Cool		

CONTRIBUTE TO A COMMUNITY SCIENCE PROJECT

If you or your parents have a smartphone, ask if it's OK to download **iNaturalist** (iOS and Android). This app is all about nature, and it's a wonderful way to keep track of—and identify your finds—and you can help science in the process.

WHAT TO DO

The way it works is simple. You sign up (you have to be 13 years old to have your own account), and then you take a photo of an animal, plant, mushroom, or the like that you spot. You then create an observation, add the photo, and click the "What Did You See?" button. The app runs the photo through a computer program that will try to identify it. The program isn't perfect, but it often helps you narrow down what you found.

Then, if you share your observation and location online, other observers (including experts) can help confirm your identification (or propose a new one). Once an observation has two identifications that are the same, it's considered "research grade," which means it can be used by real scientists!

In fact, this might happen faster than you think. Some of my friends have had scientists contact them, either because the species they photographed hadn't been recorded in that area or because they wanted a sample of the species.

Note: If you're worried about posting your location, there's an option to click "Obscured" under the app's "Geolocation" settings. This prevents people from seeing exactly where you made your observation—instead, it gives only a large range.

NATURE BINGO

Circle the nature you see, and see who gets a bingo first!

NATURE

B I N G O

DANDELION	BEE	MAMMAL	OAK LEAF	GRASS
CONIFEROUS TREE (EVERGREEN)	ROCK	MOSS	LADYBUG	CLOUD
SPIDER	ANT	FREE THE SKY SPACE	BEETLE	DECIDUOUS TREE
THE MOON	WORM	BIRD	LOG	STAR (THE SUN COUNTS!)
MUSHROOM	MAPLE LEAF	PINE CONE	BUTTERFLY	FROG

NATURE

BINGO

B	I	N	G	O
CRAB	CLAM	BUTTERFLY	GULL (SEAGULL)	BEACH GRASS
DRY SAND	WET ROCK	WRACK LINE	SNAIL	SHOREBIRD
INSECT (ANY KIND)	LADYBUG	FREE THE SKY SPACE	WET SAND	AN ANIMAL BIGGER THAN YOUR HAND
THE MOON	SOMETHING SWIMMING IN THE WATER	SMELL SALTY AIR	STAR (THE SUN COUNTS!)	ALGAE (SEAWEED)
EMPTY SHELL	SHELL WITH A LIVING CREATURE IN IT	FLOWER	CLOUD	DRY ROCK

RECORD YOUR ACTIVITIES, DISCOVERIES & FINDS HERE

If you find something neat, make a sketch to the right to help you remember details so you can compare your drawing to a field guide or another reference later.

_____

_____

_____

_____

_____

_____

_____

_____

_____

_____

_____

_____

0 inch 1 2 3 4 5 6 7 8 9 10

RECORD YOUR ACTIVITIES, DISCOVERIES & FINDS HERE

If you find something neat, make a sketch to the right to help you remember details so you can compare your drawing to a field guide or another reference later.

_____

_____

_____

_____

_____

_____

_____

_____

_____

_____

_____

_____

RECORD YOUR ACTIVITIES, DISCOVERIES & FINDS HERE

If you find something neat, make a sketch to the right to help you remember details so you can compare your drawing to a field guide or another reference later.

_____

_____

_____

_____

_____

_____

_____

_____

_____

_____

_____

_____

RECORD YOUR ACTIVITIES, DISCOVERIES & FINDS HERE

If you find something neat, make a sketch to the right to help you remember details so you can compare your drawing to a field guide or another reference later.

_____

_____

_____

_____

_____

_____

_____

_____

_____

_____

_____

RECOMMENDED READING

Barker, Margaret, and Elissa Wolfson. *Audubon Birding Adventures for Kids: Activities and Ideas for Watching, Feeding, and Housing Our Feathered Friends.* New York: Cold Spring Press. 2020.

Brandt, DeAnna. *Bird Log Kids.* Cambridge, Minnesota: Adventure Publications. 1998.

Brandt, DeAnna. *Bug Log Kids.* Cambridge, Minnesota: Adventure Publications. 2017.

Brandt, DeAnna. *Nature Log Kids.* Cambridge, Minnesota: Adventure Publications. 1998 .

Brandt, DeAnna. *Rock Log Kids.* Cambridge, Minnesota: Adventure Publications. 2018.

Burns, Diane; Dendy, Leslie; and Mel Boring (Author). *Fun with Nature: Take Along Guide.* Lanham, Maryland: Cooper Square Publishing, 1998.

Daniels, Jaret C. *Backyard Bugs: An Identification Guide to Common Insects, Spiders, and More.* Cambridge, Minnesota: Adventure Publications, 2017.

Eisner, Thomas. *For Love of Insects.* Cambridge, Mass: Belknap Press, 2003.

Himmelman, John. *Discovering Moths: Nighttime Jewels in Your Own Backyard.* Camden, Maine: Down East Books, 2002.

Lynch, Dan R. *Fossils for Kids: An Introduction to Paleontology.* Cambridge, Minnesota: Adventure Publications, 2020.

Lynch, Dan R. *Rock Collecting for Kids: An Introduction to Geology.* Cambridge, Minnesota: Adventure Publications, 2018.

Poppele, Jonathan. *Night Sky: A Field Guide to the Constellations.* Cambridge, Minnesota: Adventure Publications, 2018.

Sayre, April Pulley. *Touch a Butterfly: Wildlife Gardening with Kids.* Boulder, Colorado: Roost Books, 2013.

Tomsen, Amanda. *Backyard Adventure: Get Messy, Get Wet, Build Cool Things, and Have Tons of Wild Fun! 51 Free-Play Activities.* North Adams, Massachusetts: Storey Publishing, 2019.

Torino, Stacy, and Ken Keffer. *Bird Braniacs: Activity Journal and Log Book for Young Birders.* Apex, North Carolina: Cornell Lab Publishing Group, 2016.

GLOSSARY

Biome A community of animals and plants that live in a specific kind of climate and environment.

Birder Someone who enjoys observing birds.

Chemical Element One of the 92 naturally occurring chemicals such as oxygen, carbon, etc., that make up all matter on Earth.

Classification What scientists do when they group the life forms they study into different categories based on many different characteristics and traits.

Climate Long-term patterns in the weather.

Commodities Farm products, such as corn and soybeans, that are sold worldwide.

Conglomerate A rock that is made up of a bunch of different rocks stuck together.

Conifer A tree that produces seeds by cones; most conifers, but not all, are **evergreen** (see below).

Ecosystem All the interactions between living and nonliving things within a particular area.

Evergreen A tree that doesn't lose its leaves but instead stays green all winter.

Extirpated Another word for animals being wiped out from their original habitat.

Glaciers Huge rivers of ice that once covered much of the Northeast, creating a lot of the topography (landscapes) we see (or don't see) today.

Hypothesis A guess based on information you already know.

Ice age One of many periods in Earth's history of prolonged cold and glacial activity. The last ice age ended around 10,000 years ago.

Igneous Describes a rock formed by a volcano or lava cooling on the earth's surface.

GLOSSARY

Introduced Brought to an area instead of occurring there naturally (example: cows in the U.S.).

Invasive Describes introduced species (see above) that outcompete native animals, harming the ecosystem.

Invertebrates Animals without backbones.

Killing Frost When temperatures reach around 28 degrees Fahrenheit, it gets cold enough to freeze the water in some plants, killing the ones that are sensitive to cold.

Latitude How far north or south a person or place is of the equator; the equator is at a latitude of 0 degrees, and the North Pole is 90 degrees North.

Longitude How far east or west a person or place is of the prime meridian, which is at a longitude of 0 degrees.

Metamorphic Describes a rock that has changed under intense heat and/or pressure.

Metamorphosis The process that causes some animals to change body plans completely from young to adult.

Mineral An individual element or combination of elements that is consistent throughout and that has solidified, or crystallized.

Mohs Hardness Scale The relative scale of mineral hardness, from the softest (talc, 1) to the hardest (diamond, 10).

Mutualistic Beneficial for every organism in a relationship.

Native Describes an animal, plant, or other organism that is found naturally in an area.

Nonnative Describes an animal, plant, or other organism that isn't naturally found in an area. Note that not all nonnative species are invasive (see page 28).

Organism A living creature: plant, animal, fungus, microbe, etc.

Parasite A life form that feeds on or otherwise depends on another life form.

Plankton Microscopic aquatic plants and animals.

Phenology The study of the seasons and other natural cycles over time.

Rock A combination of two or more minerals.

Saprobes Mushrooms that feed on dead or dying material (often wood or plant parts).

Scientific Name Because there are so many different plants and animals and other life forms, scientists give each one an official scientific name, usually derived from Latin or Greek and put in *italic text* to make it stand out. Scientific names have two parts: a **genus name,** which is like an organism's last name and which it shares with others, and a **species name,** which is like its first name. So if you want to talk to a scientist about the American Robin, *Turdus migratorius* (yep, that's its real scientific name) is how scientists all around the world would recognize it.

Sedimentary Describes a rock that forms as particles of soil and minerals accumulate in layers over long periods of time.

Summer Solstice The longest day of the year, when Earth is pointed most directly at the sun; in the northern hemisphere, the summer solstice occurs in late June.

Temperate Describes an environment where there are long periods (summer!) where the weather is warm.

Threatened On its way to becoming extinct.

Toxic Poisonous.

Vascular Tissue Specialized plant parts that carry nutrients that plants need, such as water and sugar.

Weather The day-to-day observations of temperature, rainfall and snowfall, cloud cover, etc.

Winter Solstice The shortest day of the year, when Earth is pointed farthest away from the sun; in the northern hemisphere, the winter solstice occurs in late December.

Wrack Line The line of plant and pebble debris created by the high tide.

QUICK QUIZ ANSWERS

Page 5: Connecticut: Hartford; Delaware: Dover; Maine: Augusta; Maryland: Annapolis; Massachusetts: Boston; New Hampshire: Concord; New Jersey: Trenton; New York: Albany; Pennsylvania: Harrisburg; Rhode Island: Providence; Vermont: Montpelier

Page 7: Trees!

Page 9: B. Red Pine

Page 11: 1. Oak, 2. Sugar Maple, 3. Hickory, 4. Tulip Poplar

Page 13: D. All of these things

Page 15: E. All of them

Page 16: B. White-Tailed Deer (state animal of Pennsylvania and New Hampshire)

Page 29: C. Cow

Page 51: A. Soybeans, B. Corn, C. Cranberries, D. Blueberries, E. Potatoes

Page 53: C. Mountain Laurel

Page 94: B. Belemnite and E. *Hadrosaurus foulkii*

Page 107: Dog-Day Cicada, Painted Skimmer, and Monarch Butterfly

Page 112: The third insect is a bee. The first one is a Hoverfly, and the second one is an Ornate Snipe Fly.

CROSSWORD ANSWERS

Geology & Gemstones, page 100:

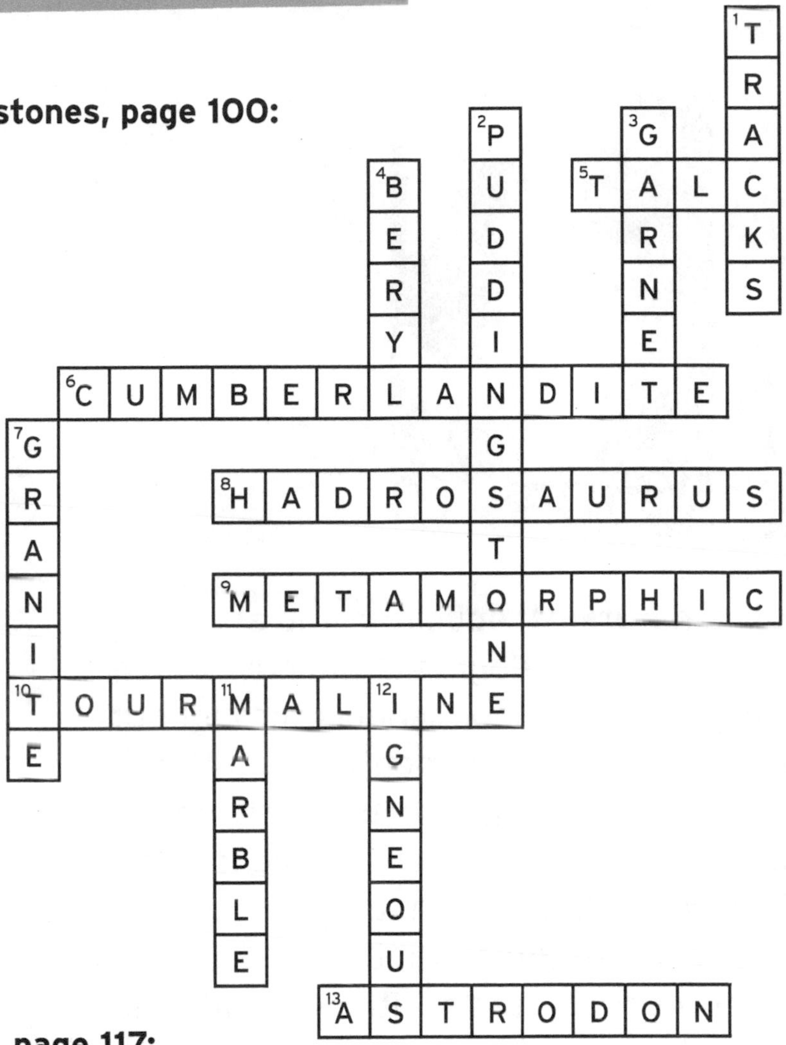
1 TRACKS
2 PUDDINGSTONE
3 GARNET
4 BERYL
5 TALC
6 CUMBERLANDITE
7 GRANITE
8 HADROSAURUS
9 METAMORPHIC
10 TOURMALINE
11 MARBLE
12 IGNEOUS
13 ASTRODON

Bugs & Insects, page 117:

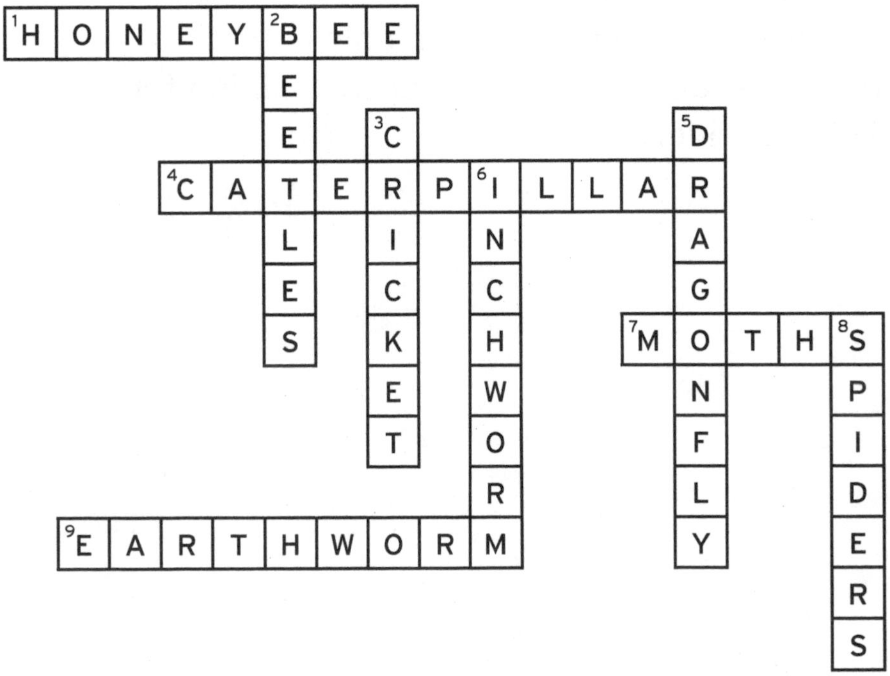
1 HONEYBEE
2 BEETLES
3 CRICKET
4 CATERPILLAR
5 DRAGONFLY
6 INCHWORM
7 MOTHS
8 SPIDERS
9 EARTHWORM

ABOUT THE AUTHOR

Susan D. Schenck is a naturalist, educator, and artist. After earning an undergraduate degree in biology, Susan taught at several residential outdoor schools throughout the U.S., including earning an environmental education teaching certificate while teaching in northern Minnesota. She recently moved to Pennsylvania from Rhode Island, where she taught classes at Casey Farm and co-founded the Ocean State Bird Club's Youth Birders Initiative. Susan loves exploring all the different ecosystems with her students!

At the time of this writing, Susan and her husband, Matt, call northwestern Pennsylvania home. Susan enjoys birding and keeping a nature journal, and she's currently training for a century (100-mile) bike ride.

ACKNOWLEDGMENTS

Thanks to my parents, who encouraged me to get outside as much as possible. Thanks to my husband, Matt, for his encouragement and inspiration. Thanks to my mentors and friends from the following residential outdoor schools: Glen Helen Outdoor Education Center, Camp Jekyll and Rock Eagle 4-H Centers, and Wolf Ridge Environmental Learning Center.

DEDICATION

This book is for all you curious kids out there.
Keep exploring!

PHOTO CREDITS

All photos listed below are copyright of their respective photographers.

Front and back cover images used under license from Shutterstock. Front cover: **Ginger Wang:** Baltimore Checkerspot Butterfly with closed wings; **Paul Reeves Photography:** Baltimore Checkerspot Butterfly with open wings; **Steve Byland:** Eastern Bluebird; **Steve Mann:** ruler; **Svetlana Foote:** Monarch Caterpillar; **Vitaly Korovin:** magnifying glass and pencil; **watin:** Black-Eyed Susan **Back cover: Svetlana Foote:** Monarch Caterpillar

Interior images:
Jon Dawson: 59 (Hoye-Crest, MD); **Jimmy S. Emerson, DVM:** 59 (Delaware–Pennsylvania state line), 60 (Jerimoth Hill, RI); **Kevin McCartney:** *Pertica quadrifaria* on pp. 27 and 94; **Brett Ortler:** 40, 43 (robin's nest), 68 (Wild Geranium, Butterfly Bush, and Cardinal Flower), 70, 71, 75, 80, 102 (White-Lined Sphinx Moth, Monarch Butterfly, and Viceroy Butterfly), 103 (House Fly, Margined Calligrapher Fly, Potato Beetle, Six-Spotted Tiger Beetle, and Goldenrod Soldier Beetle), 104 (Bumblebee, Giant Ichneumon Wasp, and Carpenter Ant), 105 (Leaf Hopper and Stink Bug), 106 (Cobweb Spider and Bronze Jumping Spider), 107 (Monarch Butterfly), 108, 109 (both), 111 (Rusty-Patched Bumblebee), 112 (Ornate Snipe Fly), 113, 114, 115 (both), 118 (both), 119, 127 (both), 128 (bottom left and right), 139, 141 **Matt Schenck:** 45 (Springtime Darner), 48 (Dark-Eyed Junco and Harlequin Duck), 102 (Pearl Crescent), 104 (Springtime Darner, Painted Skimmer, and Powdered Dancer), 107 (Painted Skimmer) **Susan Schenck:** Ladybug on pp. 18, 20 and 26, Pink Lady's Slipper on pp. 26 and 44, 55 (all), 56 (all), 57 (all), 99

Page 92 (Charlotte Whale) From "On a skeleton of a whale in the provincial museum, Halifax, Nova Scotia; with notes on the fossil cetacea of North America," by George H. Perkins, in *Proceedings of the Nova Scotian Institute of Science* 12 (1910): 1906–1910.

Images used under license from Shutterstock: Abishek Michael: 54 (Glasswort); **adempercem:** 17 (White Oak); **Adrian _am13:** 123 (Coral Fungi); **Agnieszka Bacal:** 22 (violet); **Akvals:** Dog-Day Cicada on pp. 105 and 107; **Alexander Image:** striped bass on pp. 17 and 22; **Alexander Sviridov:** 28 (earthworms); **Amka Artist:** 19 (Knobbed Whelk); **Anastasia Bulanova:** Smoky Quartz on pp. 26 and 93; **Anastasiia Malinich:** 36; **Andreas Juergensmeier:** 130; **Andriy Kananovych:** 96 and 97 (all); **Antonina Potapenko:** 14 (bottom); **Arctic ice:** 95 (top); **Arlift Atoz2205:** 19 (Blue Violet); **Armin Staudt:** 123 (Giant Puffball); **Arvind Balaraman:** 20 (Snapping Turtle); **azure1:** 95 (bottom); **Barbara Storms:** 111 (Sweat Bee); **Bee_acg:** Hadrosaur on pp. 19 and 86; **Beekeepx:** 43 (Sugar Maple Flower); **Bob Pool:** Isopod on pp. 106 and 107; **Bogdan Ionescu:** 122 (Oyster Mushroom), 123 (Dead Man's Fingers), 124 (Chocolate Tube Slime Mold); **Bonnie Taylor Barry:** 20 (Eastern Bluebird); **Bradley D. Saum:** 21 (Eastern Hemlock); **Bradley Van Reenan:** 44 (Garter Snake); **Breck P. Kent:** *Eurypterus remipes* on pp. 20 and 88, grossular garnet on pp. 25 and 87, marble on p. 91; **Brian A. Wolf:** Baltimore Oriole on pp. 17 and 65; **Brian Lasenby:** 26 (White Birch); **brizmaker:** 79; **BW Folsom:** 22 (Quahog); **CampSmoke:** 106 (millipede); **CEW:** 69; **Cheryl Thomas:** 45 (Monarch Butterfly); **Chris Alcock:** 45 (cicada); **Christian Musat:** 20 (beaver); **Claire Anna Jones:** 111 (Squash Bee); **Claire Prendergast:** 12 (left); **Clara Bastian:** 29 (cow); **ClubhouseArts:** 11 (Sugar Maple leaves); **Colin D. Young:** 59 (New York high point); **consciouslygrowing:** 8 (bottom); **Cora Unk Photo:** 123 (Earthball); **coxy58:** 131 (Periwinkle Snails); **Cynthia Shirk:** 52 (Jack-in-the-Pulpit); **Dan Logan:** puddingstone on pp. 23 and 89; **Daniel Prudek:** honeybee on pp. 19, 25, 27 and 104;

Danita Delimont: Baltimore Checkerspot on p. 17, Eastern Swallowtail Butterfly on pp. 44 and 102; **Daria Plotnikova:** 53 (New York Aster); **David Byron Keener:** 46 (American Goldfinch); **David R. Duncan:** 17 (Black-Eyed Susan); **Diane E. Ennis:** 105 (grasshopper); **dibrova:** 23 (American Elm); **divedog:** 54 (Eel Grass); **Dotted Yeti:** *Eubrontes giganteus* on pp. 24 and 88; **dwcreations:** 102 (Cecropia Moth); **Ed Connor:** 30; **Edward Fielding:** Sugar Maple on pp. 9 and 29; **ehrlif:** 52 (trillium); **Eileen Kumpf:** 112 (Flower Fly); **Elliotte Rusty Harold:** 54 (American Beach Grass), 111 (Carpenter Bee), bumblebee on pp. 111 and 112; **Eric Isselee:** 24 (European Mantis); **Erik Agar:** 104 (Ebony Jewelwing), 112 (Bee Fly); **Esposito Photography:** 35; **Flower _Garden:** 52 (Mayapple); **Formatoriginal:** 132 (Blue Mussels); **FotoCat99:** 47 (Poison Ivy); **FotoLot:** 123 (False Morel); **fotolotos:** 39 (lilacs); **Frank Reiser:** Asian Shore Crab on pp. 28 and 133; **Frank DeBonis:** Ghost Pipe on pp. 46 and 53; **Frode Jacobsen:** 103 (Carrion Beetle); **galitsin:** 106 (worm); **galsand:** 138; **Garrett Gibson:** 28 (European Starling); **GenOne360:** 132 (horseshoe crab); **Geoffrey Kuchera:** 18 (Gray Fox); **Gerry Bishop:** 77 (top), 124 (Raspberry Slime Mold), 131 (Knobbed Whelk); **Gilbert S. Grant:** oysters on pp. 24 and 132; **Gnilenkov Aleksey:** 103 (Robber Fly); **godi photo:** 124 (Wolf's Milk Slime); **Gregg Williams:** American Goldfinch on pp. 19 and 62; **Grigorii Pisotsckii:** 25 (Red Clover), 122 (Birch Polypore); **guentermanaus:** 52 (Joe-Pye Weed); **Henri Koskinen:** garnet on pp. 20, 24, and 87, 122 (Milk-White Toothed Polypore), 123 (Bear's Head Tooth); **Henrik Larsson:** 104 (Yellow Jacket), 121 (Witch's Hat); **HHelene:** 132 (Soft-Shell Clam); **Holly Damann:** 18 (American Holly); **Ibe van Oort:** sillimanite and belemnite on pp. 18 and 84; **Ihor Hvozdetskyi:** 106 (Goldenrod Crab Spider); **Imran Ashraf:** 52 (columbine); **Inachis Projekt:** 134 (top middle); **IrinaK:** 133 (Hermit Crab); **Isabel Eve:** 103 (Broad-Necked Root Borer); **J. C. McConnell Morphart Creation:** Ecphora on pp. 17 and 85; **jadimages:** 52 (Pink Lady's Slipper); **James Griffiths Photo:** Maine high point on pp. 58 and 61; **Jamie Oakley:** 33; **Jarous:** 18 (horseshoe crab; **Jason Kostansek:** 44 (Canada Geese); **JayL:** Mountain Laurel on pp. 21 and 24; **Jeff Holcombe:** 52 (Starflower), 54 (Saltmarsh Cordgrass); **Jillian Cain Photography:** 78 (osprey nest); **João Virissimo:** Channeled Whelk on pp. 18 and 131; **Joel Trick:** 77 (Monarch Butterfly); **Jolanda Aalbers:** 23 (Two-Spotted Lady Beetle), 121 (Laccaria); **Jovana Kuzmanovic:** 106 (centipede); **Julia Zavalishina:** 121 (Red Fly Agaric); **K. Steve Cope:** 14 (top); **Karel Bock:** 42 (Skunk Cabbage); **Kazu Inoue:** 54 (Beach Pea); **Kichigin:** 123 (puffball spores); **KrimKate:** 82 (rhodonite); **Kristi Blokhin:** 78 (Downy Woodpecker); **Kristina Postnikova:** 51 (potato field); **lecsposure:** 137; **Lee Ellsworth:** 52 (Canada Mayflower); **Lia Caldas:** 134 (top left); **Liene Kozachenko:** 123 (False Truffles); **Lijuan Guo:** 51 (cranberry bog); **Lisa Kolbenschlag:** horse on pp. 19 and 25; **Lost Mountain Studio:** 131 (Moon Snail); **Luka Hercigonja:** 47 (Goldenrod); **lunamarina:** Blue Hen on pp. 18 and 64; **Lynn Gedeon:** 43 (trillium); **M Rose:** Brook Trout on pp. 19, 20, 21, 25, and 26; **M. Schuppich:** 53 (Queen Anne's Lace); **M. E. Parker:** 133 (Ghost Crab); **Marc Bruxelle:** 49 (maple sap bucket; **Marc Goldman:** 28 (House Sparrow); **Margaret M Stewart:** 49 (Black Bear); **Martin Fowler:** 28 (Garlic Mustard); **Matt Jeppson:** 102 (Giant Silk Caterpillar); **Matthew R. McClure:** Bay Scallop on pp. 20 and 132; **Mazur Travel:** 39 (red apples); **McCarthy's PhotoWorks:** 98; **Melinda Fawver:** 11 (oak), 23 (Eastern Garter Snake), 105 (Northern Bush Katydid); **Michael G. Mill:** Black-Capped Chickadee on pp. 23, 27 and 63; **Michael S. Moncrief:** 124 (Dog Vomit Slime Mold); **Michael Siluk:** 116; **Michael Tatman:** 42 (Red-Winged Blackbird); **michal812:** 82 (granite); **Michiel de Wit:** 25 (Northern Leopard Frog); **Mike Truchon:** 52 (Dutchman's Breeches);

NATURE JOURNALS FOR KIDS
from
ADVENTURE PUBLICATIONS

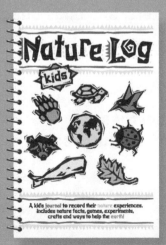

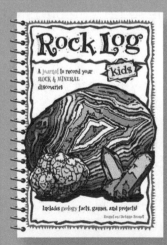

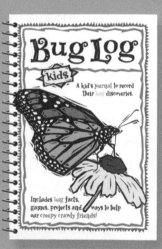

- Guided journaling pages
- Fascinating information
- Fun activities for the family
- Photo and art pages

SAFETY NOTE

Nature is wonderful and amazing, and it's certainly nothing to be afraid of, especially if you use common sense and take precautions.

This guide is intended for backyards and green spaces in the Northeast. These places should be pretty safe by definition, but make sure to have an adult with you when you're outside to supervise the activities in this book. And when you're outside, don't reach where you can't see, and be aware of potentially dangerous animals like bees, wasps, venomous spiders or snakes, and bothersome plants such as poison ivy or poison sumac or oak. There really aren't all that many of these creatures or plants, but if you know they can be found in your area, or if you have allergies (to bees, for instance), it's important to simply be aware that they may be out there.

The best way to stay safe is to keep your distance from wild animals, avoid handling wildlife, and take photos or draw sketches instead. Also, wear gloves, the right clothing for the weather, and sunscreen (as needed), and pay attention to the weather and any potentially unsafe surroundings. *Remember:* You're responsible for your safety.

A quick note about the internet: In this guide, sometimes we suggest going online to learn more about a topic or to contribute information in some way. If you're under 13 years old, please check in with an adult first to make sure it's OK.

An especially important note: Don't use this book to help you identify which wild plants, berries, fruits, or mushrooms are safe to eat. Please leave these for the birds, critters, and bugs out there.

Edited by Brett Ortler

Cover and book design by Fallon Venable

**Backyard Nature and Science Workbook: Northeast
Fun Activities and Experiments That Get Kids Outdoors**
Copyright © 2021 by Susan D. Schenck
Published by Adventure Publications
An imprint of AdventureKEEN
310 Garfield Street South
Cambridge, Minnesota 55008
(800) 678-7006
www.adventurepublications.net
All rights reserved
Printed in the United States of America
ISBN 978-1-64755-170-4

CPSIA information can be obtained
at www.ICGtesting.com
Printed in the USA
JSHW020451120421
13423JS00004B/4

9 781647 551704